CARL KIGER: THE MAN BEYOND THE MURDER

ROBERT SCHRAGE

Carl Kiger: The Man Beyond the Murder

ISBN: 978-0-9816123-6-2

Author: Robert Schrage

Original cover photo courtesy of the <u>Kentucky Post</u>. Cover artwork by The Merlot Group.

ISBN: 978-0-9816123-6-2

Published by:

The Merlot Group, LLC, P.O. Box 302, Covington KY 41012-0302

(859) 743-1003, www.merlotgroup.com

The Merlot Group

This book is dedicated to my beloved son Andrew J. Schrage (1989-2011), who taught me so much. He was a great friend to many. Andrew was honest, civil, and hard working. He loved life. I love him and miss him everyday.

I wish to thank the following people for help with this book: Bridget Striker, Ann Schrage, Tracy Denham, Jim Kiger, Shawn Masters, Jerod Theobald, Emilie Nerl, Will Terwort, Asa Rouse, Bruce Ferguson, Jenny Gridley, Dave Schroeder, the Kenton County Public Library, the Boone County Public Library, Ed Currin, Matt Becher, Iymi Bolden, and Richard Roeding.

Preface

In Boone County, Kentucky, the Kiger Family is most well known for the events that took place on August 17th, 1943 at Rosegate Farm. Nearly seventy years and several news articles, a book and two plays later, speculation and controversy still swirl around the night Carl Kiger and his six year old son, Jerry died. At the center of that notorious night was Carl's fifteen year old daughter, Joan, who was later placed on trial for the shooting deaths of both Carl and Jerry.

On that fateful Tuesday night, Carl and his wife Jennie, along with their two youngest children Joan and Jerry were asleep in their beds when someone shot and killed both Carl and Jerry, wounding Jennie in the hip. Joan, unharmed, drove the family car to the neighbors to get help. When Boone County Sheriff Jake Williams arrived at the scene, the house was full of both Kenton and Grant County officials. According to officials at the scene, the house was locked up tight with no evidence of intruders.

Carl Kiger was considered a suspicious man and kept three pistols in the house - two downstairs in his study and one in his upstairs bedroom, under his pillow. He insisted all the doors and windows of Rosegate were kept shut and locked at night - even in the heat of summer. Why was Carl Kiger so paranoid about his family's safety? No one knows for certain. However, rumors have alluded to Kiger's mob connections as Vice-Mayor of Covington. After the deaths, $1440 in cash was found in the house, speculated to be slot-machine pay off money.

On December 14th, 1943 the Boone County Grand Jury indicted both Joan and Jennie Kiger for the *willful murder* of Carl and Jerry Kiger. The case was brought to trial in the Burlington Court House on December 16, 1943. Joan, now 16, was tried as an adult for the death of little Jerry; her mother to stand trial later. Although a motive was still debated, Prosecuting Attorney Vincent sought the death penalty. Joan was defended by prominent attorney Sawyer A. Smith. Judge Ward Jager presided over the five day trial.

During the trial, Joan's tendency towards night terrors- very intense and seemingly real nightmares- was brought to light. Apparently, Joan inherited the affliction from her father. The theory was that Joan thought she heard gun shots in the house and was defending against an intruder. Experts were brought in to testify whether or not gun shots would have awoken Joan from a dream state. Joan testified that she fired at shadowy figures that she thought were shooting at her. It was shown that the gun that was used to kill Jerry Joan gave to Jennie before leaving the house. Schiffer states, "the defense hinged on whether the jury would buy into Smith's defense that Joan was not in her right mind when she did the shooting and therefore not responsible."

After a four hour deliberation, the jury found no proven motives for the murder of Jerry Kiger. The twelve Boone County men, found Joan Kiger not guilty. As a result of the not guilty verdict, the prosecution dropped all charges against both Joan and her mother. Without the first conviction, there was no motivation to try the other cases.

In 1943, it was hard to conceive that a "nice girl" would kill her family. Carl Kiger's alleged political connections led to speculation that the Mob killed Kiger and set Joan up as the scapegoat for the murders. In the years that have followed the trial, the community has remained divided about Joan's role in her father and brother's deaths. Fellow students have remained adamant that Joan would not have knowingly killed her family. Others firmly believe that Joan was not as innocent as she seemed and that she got away with murder. In Boone County, the murders and subsequent trial remain one of the most discussed single events in Boone County history. Regardless of motives or guilty parties, one fact remains constant; the Kiger Family was destroyed that night in August of 1943.

Note: Built in the nineteenth century, Rosegate Farm with its 20 acres was located in the little town of Devon, along Dixie Highway just south of Florence, Kentucky. The large two-story house was demolished in 2005.

- Bridget K. Striker, Local History Coordinator
Boone County Public Library

INTRODUCTION

More than a century removed from the youth of Carl Kiger, the
quiet road to Saint John's Cemetery is sprawled with modern homes. The
temperature is well below freezing as I reach the entrance to the old
cemetery about a mile from Dixie Highway. Just a few miles from
downtown Cincinnati and West Covington, grave markers are covered
with a couple inches of snow. In the cemetery, the road is not cleared of
snow and the only place to park is in the middle of the road, or risk
slipping off or getting stuck. The graves of young Jerry Kiger and his
father Carl are somewhere under a snow covered marker. Searching, I
clear the snow from around fifteen headstones. Markers to the name
Hoelscher indicate the Kigers lie nearby. The one covering the boy and
his father is finally unveiled with its names jumping out as if they were old
friends. Son Jerry 1937-1943; Father Carl C. 1893-1943; and Mother
Jennie C. 1893-1979, reads the single marker under the name Kiger. The
final resting place of two murder victims and a wounded mother that lived
36 years after being shot, lie near the cemetery entrance, silent to the story
that became one of the most famous homicides in the region's history and
at the time, a national story.

Their four bedroom summer home, called Rosegate, was situated
on twenty beautiful acres and consisted of a large lake, several barns,
chicken coops, and a spectacular green landscape. Much controversy
would surround Carl Kiger's summer home including accusations of it
being bought with mob money; questions of whether his legal residency
was really in Covington where he served as vice-mayor; and most
importantly, the double murder taking place involving the most powerful
elected official in Covington and his son. Years later, the home would be
put up for auction including well over two hundred personal items of this

once prominent family. Today, the house is gone and nothing would tell a passerby of the tragedy that happened there. Accusations abound this house was bought with money supplied by the Cleveland Syndicate. Kiger bought it because he could. He kept it clean and it was a haven for his children. According to Kiger expert Asa Rouse, it was perhaps the most beautiful home in Boone County at the time. It was well maintained and clean.

The murder of Carl Kiger and his six-year old son Jerry, not only ended the heyday of a beautiful plantation-like homestead, but a political career steeped in controversy. From the time he was first elected to the Covington City Commission, Kiger had one objective—to throw out the city commission and mayor and replace it with his anti-establishment coalition. From 1937 until his death, Kiger served during perhaps the most important and dynamic time in Covington history. Less than a decade before his election, Covington officially threw out the old boss system and adopted a city manager form of government. He would spend his political career without respect or support for this move. His career paralleled the Great Depression, part of World War II, and just a month after taking office, the arrival of the great flood of 1937.

Carl Kiger worked his way up from his poor West Covington neighborhood to become Covington's most powerful and controversial figure. He met and became friends with governors, senators, and a future vice-president. He shared a stage with President Roosevelt. He accomplished many goals and failed at many others. He was liked and disliked. He participated in a system dominated by political strife, favoritism, and corruption. His story is one from the old school. He served at a time situated right in the middle of a city trying to break away from the corruption of the past; and beginning a new, professional style government. At times, he was a reformer and at others as old school as it gets. He could be the equivalent of Cincinnati's Boss Cox on one hand, and on the other, an advocate who implemented efficient and necessary financial reforms.

Carl Kiger was an enigma. His murder is well-known. This is the story of Carl Kiger the politician and man. You may like him; you may not. Maybe you don't know what to think. Regardless, his story is a lesson in civics, history, controversy, influence peddling, and murder.

CHAPTER 1

Born and raised in the west end of Covington, Kiger long desired to become a city leader. He was ambitious and developed as a central political theme later described by his colleagues, as always "zealous to see that the tax payer's money was spent judiciously and wisely."[1] Many describe him as a champion of the poor and the working class. The west end of Covington is a working class neighborhood, with several churches and corner grocery stores. It was here that Carl Kiger grew up playing in the streets and perhaps the nearby Devou Park, with its tremendous views of downtown Cincinnati. Kiger was raised at 519 Crescent Avenue in a spot now occupied by the parking lot of the Cork N Bottle liquor store. The urban environment in which Kiger grew up lies less than a mile from downtown Cincinnati and the houses are tightly woven together in the hilliest parts of Covington. He had a perfect view of downtown Cincinnati from his house. Today, much of the old Crescent Avenue housing is demolished and has been replaced by newer condos. However, several demolished buildings have never been replaced and lots remain vacant on both sides of the road. The house Kiger grew up in is long gone; as is the house he would eventually own on the same street and live in at the time of his death. In 1900, three family members who lived at 519 Crescent Avenue were working: Carl's father, William J., was a tobacconist and his two brothers, John H. and William, were both mill hands. Carl's mother, Jennie, raised the children.

According to Jim Kiger, great nephew to Carl, the Kiger family emigrated from Germany around the 1860's. German immigration was very prominent in Northern Kentucky and Cincinnati and Kentucky in general. The first Germans came before the Revolutionary War through Virginia, the Carolinas, and Pennsylvania, according to Don Heinrich

Tolzmann. [2] Their main route was through the Cumberland Gap, but later in the 19th century they came from Germany directly and, traveling down the Ohio River, settled in Northern Kentucky and Cincinnati. Other prominent cities included Milwaukee and St. Louis, creating according to Tolzmann, the "German Triangle". Like most areas, the Germans in Covington lived in groups or neighborhoods together. Businesses such as bakeries, brewers, cigar makers, tailors, and wood workers, would develop in these communities. Covington was no different and members of the Kiger family worked in some of these professions. They were also religious, as were most German immigrants.

The Kigers of West Covington worshiped at St. Aloysius Church located at the southeast corner of West 7th Street and Bakewell. Carl attended St Aloysius School at least through the eighth grade. Jim Kiger doesn't think he graduated high school. They were poor and the red-headed Carl had to get a job to support the family. Mass was in German and Carl had to learn the language if for no other reason than his dad spoke German. As important, the nuns at the school taught in German. St. Aloysius was one of the largest German churches and was founded in 1865. A year later they commissioned noted architect Louis Picket to design the permanent church.[3] In 1867, a "grandiose Romanesque Revival Style Church, with a pointed Gothic Spire"[4] was dedicated. Later elaborate stained glass windows made in Germany were added, as well as, the construction of "the famous Grotto of Lourges of France in its basement featuring exquisite hand-carved statues imported from Germany that depicted the first miracle of Lourges."[5] On May 16, 1985, lightning struck the beautiful church destroying the building. The parish was then merged with Mother of God.

Growing up in Covington certainly included playing ball in the streets for young Carl Kiger. Like most kids, particularly in the summer, he would likely play all day until called by bell or whistle for supper. After supper, it was back to the streets. There was much to do. According to the census of 1900, the population of Covington at that time was 42,938. Carl Kiger was seven. Ten years later, the population was 53,270. There was no shortage of kids with which to play. Getting in the way of constant play was, of course, the need to get a job, which after the eighth grade was the fate for many of the immigrants of Covington.

Just a few blocks away from St Aloysius Church stood St Patrick's Parish, one of the largest Irish churches in the region. It stood on the northwest corner of Philadelphia and Elm Streets. One family attending St Patrick's was the Hoelschers and their daughter Jennie. The Hoelschers lived just up the street at 858 Philadelphia Street. Founded in 1870, the church constructed its beautiful building in 1872. Ninety-five years later, affected by the flight to the suburbs and the opening of the 5th Street exit of I-75 in 1963, the church would close and would later merge with nearby St. Aloysius. St. Patrick's Church was demolished for a gas station the next year.[6]

Jennie would grow up in St Patrick's Church and eventually marry a parishioner of nearby St Aloysius. They were married at St. Aloysius on August 16, 1919. Jennie and Carl would continue living in Covington and eventually made plans to raise a family. Jennie, a homemaker, and salesman Carl would become well-known in the political world of Covington. At this time, their first three children were baptized at St. Aloysius: Joseph Charles on August 19, 1920; John William on May 23, 1923; and Joan Marie on August 28, 1927. The Kigers were living at 807 Main Street. While living on Main Street, Carl's mother died and willed the house on Crescent Avenue. It was not worth much.

Asa Rouse, a well respected Northern Kentucky lawyer who has studied the Kiger murders, says Carl Kiger doted on his kids. "They were well behaved kids and the "nuns of St Aloysius told the family Joan was well behaved and all students should be as polite and diligent as her."[7] Joan loved her little brother Jerry and would take him anywhere she could. The tragedy that eventually struck with Joan putting a bullet through young Jerry's head was still many years away. Like Joan, Carl also suffered from night terrors and, according to Rouse; he would go out in the yard at Rosegate and shoot his gun in the air, never waking up. Years later, Joan's high school classmates would say they never heard about her nightmares. They would describe her as a cheerful, normal, and loveable girl. Some folks claimed the Kigers were the happiest family they knew. Eight years after Joan was born, the strong speaking Carl Kiger made his attempt to launch a political career that would last less than a decade. The family secret of night terrors would stop the promising career in its tracks. The loveable daughter would go on trial for murder.

---

[1] Resolution R 33-44

[2] Northern Kentucky Encyclopedia, University of Kentucky Press, 2009

[3] Covington, Images of America, Arcadia Publishing, 2003

[4] Northern Kentucky Encyclopedia, University of Kentucky Press, 2009

[5] Northern Kentucky Encyclopedia, University of Kentucky Press, 2009

[6] Northern Kentucky Encyclopedia, University of Kentucky Press, 2009

[7] Interview with Asa Rouse, September 2011.

CHAPTER 2

Located on the northeast corner of Third and Court Streets, the Covington City Building stood grand through much of the history of the City of Covington, Kentucky. Today the site serves as a parking lot and on Sundays when the Cincinnati Bengals are at home, is filled with tailgaters. Founded in 1815 on the banks of the Ohio River, Covington has seen several city halls. From 1900 until it was demolished in 1970, the second Kenton County Courthouse served as the Covington City Building.[8] Like any city building, some of the most important history can be found in the daily activities of the local officials as they went about governing and leading their community. In Covington, one of the most interesting times was in the years leading up to the World War II and the first few years of the great conflict. The years saw a city struggling financially, controversy on how to grow and provide services, civil service fights, corruption, and a takeover of City Hall by a coalition of self-described reformers. The leader of the new coalition, Carl Kiger, would not see all his reforms and ambitions achieved. However, he was about to begin his journey.

1936 ELECTION

Carl Kiger first ran for elected office in 1935 and lost. He would have other set-backs and successes over the coming years. At this point in time, the anti-establishment coalition he would work so hard to create was not developed. It would be an evolutionary process developing all the way to the time of his death. Disappointed, Kiger would have to wait for the next election. He did not have to wait long. Circumstances quickly changed.

On April 6, 1936, city commissioner and former city manager O.A. Kratz died. Kratz and Kiger were political allies in the 1935 election. As a sign of the times, the Kratz vacancy stayed open for well over a year because the commission could not agree on a successor. The current commission did not want Kiger. Finally, they waited so long a special election was needed. With Kratz dead and an election necessary, Kiger seized the opportunity and sought the vacant seat. According to the <u>Kentucky Post</u>, "in announcing his candidacy, Mr. Kiger declared himself in favor of "free bridges purchased by the State" and he promised to "foster all projects that will lead to employment of citizens and promised not to be a party to secret pledges."[9] In addition, Kiger expressed his displeasure at utility companies and wanted to divorce utilities and city government. He called for the "lowest possible rates for gas, electric, transportation, and phone service."[10] These were the political themes most important to Kiger and he would champion them throughout his entire political career. So much so, each campaign sounded at times like the last.

Well-established political corruption ran rampant in Northern Kentucky during this time. The Cleveland Syndicate ran much of Campbell and Kenton counties, eventually buying "the ultra plush Beverly Hills Supper Club near Newport, Kentucky and the Coney Island Race Track in Cincinnati, renaming it River Downs."[11] The Syndicate was a very powerful family that spread its reach across the country including Northern Kentucky. Former Boone County Judge/Executive, Bruce Ferguson, an excellent historian, grew up in Covington. He described gambling as "wide open in Covington and most bars had slot machines." At this point in time, any crackdown of gambling was far off. Jim Kiger says, "It was the times. The mob dealt with people that did not go along." He added, "It was a time where any politician not on the take, would not get elected. Money was king. Even the people handing out campaign flyers at the polls were paid." Kentucky eventually stopped the distribution of campaign materials at poll sites. However, back in the day it was nice to know who was voting and who was not. Paying for votes and paying drivers to get individuals to the polls was common.

Not only was the mob influential at the time of Kiger's political start, but so were contractors who loved to influence city business. Jobs went to political friends.   Despite reforms passed in the last ten years, this was the Covington in which Kiger launched his political career.
On September 29, 1936, the <u>Kentucky Post</u> asked the appropriate questions of the candidates given the two factions in Covington politics and corruption that was known by many:

> Whatever his connections, his associates, his support, what do I know about his business ability?
>
> Has he been a notable success or notable failure in business?
>
> What do I know of this man's honesty?
>
> Can he be trusted to vote independently?
>
> Will he place his sworn duty above so-called 'loyalty to a faction?
>
> What plans have you for improving Covington's transportation situation?
>
> Will you thoroughly investigate each budgetary expenditure before you vote on it?
>
> What do you know of municipal government?
>
> Have you any idea how the city may help to meet the juvenile delinquency problem?
>
> How can Covington be made attractive to industry?

At the same time as these questions were raised, the <u>Kentucky Post</u> re-stated their strong support for the Charter City Manager Form of Government in Covington and Newport; freedom of bridges connecting Cincinnati and Northern Kentucky; eliminating "the forces that have made gambling, vice, and outlawry one off the most serious problems in Campbell and Kenton counties;" encouraging cultural, educational, artistic endeavors; and elimination of traffic and crossing hazards.[12]

Seven candidates announced to fill the vacant position. An October primary would narrow this down to two candidates to run for the seat in the November general election. Also running in the November general election were Franklin D. Roosevelt, who was seeking the second of his historic four terms, and Congressman Brent Spence. Several candidates discussed their support for the Charter City Manager Form of Government. Stanley Chrisman in announcing his candidacy said, "It seems to me that most candidates lose sight of the fact that under the city manager act the duties of commissioner have been limited to advising the manager in the operation of the city government.[13] A lawyer, Chrisman had been practicing law in Covington for fifteen years, and this was a direct shot at Kiger. Kiger, no big supporter of the city manager form of government, said at a campaign appearance, the other candidates talk in generalities and "the office of commissioner is one of real responsibility which he cannot discharge by leaving all its duties to the city manager." The final meeting of the primary campaign of the Bill Woeste for Covington City Commissioner Club was held the next night. The clubs for Woeste were organized in the interest of good government, said Campaign Chairman Curley Brennan.[14] The brotherhood of Locomotive Firemen and Enginemen Latonia Lodge 512 endorsed Charles McCabe for commissioner. Two candidates from the 1935 election, Joseph Schneider and William Good, jointly issued a statement endorsing Carl

Kiger for city commission. The statement stated, "We endorse Mr. Kiger because he is an independent candidate and as such best to serve the people of Covington." The statement went on to say, "What Covington needs is a commissioner who is not obligated to any group and who, as a taxpayer and a home owner, is interested in his community. He is best qualified on the issues of free bridges, industries, transportation, and unemployment."[15]

Primary day was wet and voter turnout miserable. Kenton County Clerk Sam Furste said on Election Day that "very few voters had cast their ballots early today."[16] All seven candidates just wanted to finish in the top two and advance to the November general election. Covington Mayor Knollman must have been nervous. A victory of the anti-administration faction led by Kiger would make the factions split at two and two on the commission. It would put the mayor in the position of breaking the 2-2 split with the fifth vote. On the other hand, his power would be great. Perhaps tempering what can be accomplished until the next election only a year away. As a special election to fill a vacant seat, the winning candidate in the general election would only serve one year before running again in the regular election cycle.

Election Day, Saturday, October 17, 1936, resulted in some interesting results. Charles McCabe came in first with Carl Kiger second. McCabe received 2862 votes, or approximately 38 percent; clearly out distancing Kiger's 1498, which made up just 20 percent of the vote. William Woeste received 1037 votes. McCabe received more votes than Kiger and Woeste combined. The biggest surprise, according to the Kentucky Post, was John J. Thornton, a perennial socialist candidate recently turned democrat to support President Roosevelt. He received 11.7 percent of the vote, only 158 votes behind Chrisman, the former city solicitor. A.A. Knipper finished sixth with 582 votes and Clarence Mayo finished last with 154 votes. Kiger had lost in 1935 and now finished a distant second in the 1936 primary. He would never lose again.

City Manger Theodore Kleumper released the nine-month city financial statement the Monday after the election, and reported receipts for the first nine months of 1936 were $1,206,733 compared with $1,112,839 for the first nine months of 1935. He also reported the city had under spent its budget for the year by approximately $50,000.

The general election for the Kratz seat was set with McCabe and Kiger facing off. The political alignment in Covington at this time was confusing despite the fact there were only two factions: The anti-administration group and the incumbent commissioners. Commissioner R.E. Culbertson was described by the Kentucky Post in an analysis of the primary as someone "leaning toward the opposition. The mayor is much more independent, the establishment faction believes, even though he has been supportive of their candidates.[17] The two establishment commissioners were William Beuttel, a plumber with a business on Pike Street, and Henry Meimann. Clearly, Beuttel and Meimann did not want an anti-establishment man on the commission. Kiger was clearly anti-administration and McCabe was saying he was not. Kiger had some coalition building still to do.

William Beuttel ran his plumbing business out of a building on Pike Street. Born February 14, 1890, he would rise to serve as mayor of Covington and run a very successful business. Beuttel grew up on Glenn Avenue in Latonia. As a child, his first memory was watching a circus parade and his first job was selling lemonade at a medicine show. When asked in 1922 what he would do if he was a public official he said, "Use business principles in the operation of various departments."[18] He may have graduated eighth grade, but like most kids of his generation went to work at a young age. His niece, Virginia Gridley, describes him "as a small portly man that was bright and ambitious. It was a surprise to the family that he got into politics. It was different than business." As an adult he loved to gamble and was a "wonderful poker player," according to Gridley. He loved the 404 Club, an old fashioned saloon that had gambling including on the horses in the back."[19]

Despite McCabe's clear win in the primary, it was not a given he would easily beat Kiger in the general election. There were many factors possibly playing in Kiger's favor. Of course, voter turnout was one. The turnout on a bad weather day was terrible. The November 3, 1936 general election would include President Roosevelt and Congressman Brent Spence on the ballot. This would be the first opportunity for voters to cast re-election votes for the President and his policies geared to getting the nation out of the depression. A good voter turnout could be expected and campaigns get out the vote efforts will have less of an impact with a wider total. In a local primary like this, the establishment supporters voted. On the other hand, Kiger was clearly seen as the leader of the anti-establishment group with his second place finish. Voters could only choose one candidate: McCabe or Kiger. Another factor would be which failed candidates would throw their support which way. There were early rumors Woeste would throw his support to the anti-group if he lost. Chrisman, an organization man, was very unhappy that the organization did not make him their "favorite son candidate," according to the Kentucky Post. The establishment would support McCabe, whom they had been lukewarm. The opposition would support Kiger. The stage was set for a nasty couple of weeks.

Both the Kiger and McCabe campaigns accused each other of irregularities. It was reported the Kiger campaign had asked precinct challengers to work for their campaign, as well as President Roosevelt and other democrats. These complaints were reported to have been received by John Brady, Kenton County Democratic Chairman; the party central committeeman; and Sheriff Vogt.[20] The Kiger campaign challenged that the McCabe campaign had unlawfully recruited city workers to work on his campaign for the primary and general elections. Elmer Ware, the Kiger campaign secretary, told the Kentucky Post, "There is no way precinct challengers can be kept from working for Kiger if they wished." It was reported Robert Moore, a Kiger supporter, distributed checks paid to precinct challengers and asked them to be for Kiger and President Roosevelt. Two days before the election, the Kentucky Post headline read "Paymaster Soliciting for Kiger is Charge." There were forty checks for precinct challengers and Moore allegedly gave them to Joseph Schneider for distribution. The five dollar checks came from the Kenton County Campaign Committee. One challenger said Moore refused to give her the five dollar check when she would not say she was for Kiger. Moore denied these charges and showed a Kentucky Post reporter the list of checks he had distributed and the checks he still had to pass out. He said all remaining checks would be distributed later that day. Moore did admit he asked challengers to pass out Kiger support cards if they had "no preference" in the election. According to Moore, all favored Kiger except the woman making the allegation. He also asked Schneider to pass out checks at the same time he distributed Fifth Ward certificates. Schneider asked Moore to pass out several of the certificates while he passed out checks.[21] Even if half this story is true, it indicates an early level of corruption, or at the very least, unethical behavior by today's standards.

On November 2, 1936, Kiger made his last appeal to the voters. "I am independent and my opponent has the administration backing." He added, "I have faith in the people of Covington and am willing to let them make the choice. I have committed myself on the issues and want to emphasize the fact I strongly favor a decent wage for city employees."

Turnout was heavy on Election Day. Like the day of the primary, it rained, but the presidential election certainly helped turnout. Roosevelt won Kentucky and 46 of the 48 states, only losing Vermont and Maine. Roosevelt was clearly the issue in the campaign. Voters had strong opinions. There was not a lot of neutrality with him. He was either liked or despised by the voters. He said, "There's one issue in this campaign. It's myself, and people must either be for me or against me." His opponent, Alf Landon, Governor of Kansas, was defeated in the biggest landside in the history of the country at that point in time. The people had spoken. They liked Roosevelt.

Brent Spence was born in Newport, Kentucky the day before Christmas in 1874. He served in the Kentucky Senate for four years between 1904 and 1908 and city solicitor of Newport from 1916 to 1924. Six years later he was elected to Congress. This 1936 election would return him to Congress for a fourth term. Spence, a bad public speaker was a quiet man and was known for his leadership and impartiality. He supported much of President Roosevelt's New and Fair Deal legislation. He retired in 1963 because of ill health and the I-75 Bridge over the Ohio River was named in his honor. Spence easily won his fourth term in the 1936 election receiving 16,963 votes in Covington alone.

In Kenton County, half the expected vote had been cast by 9:30 a.m. according to the Kentucky Post.[22] A record turnout was not possible because there were only 38,700 registered voters in Kenton County and the 1928 Hoover-Smith election turnout was 39,400.[23] In a somewhat close election, anti-establishment candidate Carl Kiger won election over his opponent "Mickey" McCabe who received 11,032 votes to Kiger's

11,716. Carl Kiger had achieved his dream of serving the city as an elected official. His takeover of city government had seen its first victory.

[8] Covington, Arcadia Publishing, by KCPL, 2003.

[9] Kentucky Post, September 26, 1936

[10] Kentucky Post, September 26, 1936

[11] The Rise and Fall of the Cleveland Mafia Page 134.

[12] Kentucky Post, September 29, 1936.

[13] Kentucky Post, October 7, 1936

[14] Kentucky Post, October 13, 1936

[15] Kentucky Post, October 15, 1936

[16] KY Post October 17, 1936.

[17] KY Post October 19, 1936.

[18] KY Post August 9, 1922

[19] Interview with Virginia Gridley October 17, 2011

[20] Kentucky Post November 2, 1937

[21] Kentucky Post, November 4, 1937

[22] KY Post November 4, 1936

[23] Kentucky Post November 4, 1936

CHAPTER 3

KIGER'S FIRST YEAR ON COMMISSION

Jim Kiger says it well in regards to the corruption aspects of Covington and its city government. Carl, "never ran as a reformer." He did not run or come in on a wave to "clean-up" City Hall. To succeed, he "had to be somewhat involved in it."

Carl Kiger's long wait to serve as a Covington commissioner came to being thirteen days after his election. On November 19, 1936, at his first meeting, Kiger cast his first vote, Resolution Number 6631, to authorize the mayor and city manager to execute an agreement with C. Rice Packing Company to construct a steam pipe line under Eastern Avenue. This first vote, unanimously approved, set in motion seven years of service often defined by tough politics, a natural disaster that devastated the community, restructuring at City Hall, cleaning up financial problems and growing pains of an urban community during the first years of World War II. During this first meeting, Kiger also voted to authorize the city to enter a five-year agreement with the City of Park Hills with water for their fire hydrants; an ordinance regulating junk dealers and second hand dealers, requiring them to hold items thirty days before disposing unless it was furniture, which only needed to be held two days; approval of a malt beverage license for a restaurant at 1725 Madison for five years; and deeding the right to the Latonia Refining Corporation to lay pipe in an alley between Emerson and College Avenue. In what must have been a bold move, he jumped right into controversy by introducing a resolution that the city solicitor was to prepare the necessary ordinances for the annexation of the territory occupied by Latonia Race Course and the Latonia Refining Corporation. He wanted it done at the earliest time possible. Early on, Kiger recognized the city needed more revenue and these two large businesses could provide it. The resolution was not passed, but set the stage for his first commission controversy.

The controversy quickly spread into the next commission meeting. At the meeting on November 25, 1936, a letter was presented from A.H. Buchanan, superintendent of the Latonia Refining Company. He said, "This company now has in its employment 178 persons, 137 living in Latonia and Covington, five in the town of Ft. Mitchell, two in Erlanger, two in Walton, one at Moauce (sic) Station, three in Sandfordtown, two in Kenton, four in Ludlow, six in Newport, and 13 in Cincinnati." Buchanan went on to say the "people employed from the City of Cincinnati are more technical men and our men are paid twice a month. Our total payroll from November 1, 1936 to November 15 comes to $14,209.31." Their average payroll was $30,000 per month. In his letter to the commissioners, Buchanan said when the company located its present plant, all property was outside the City of Covington and free from taxes. "We can not come into the city and pay city taxes and continue to in competition with our competitors. If this property is annexed, we will be compelled to suspend operations, thus cutting off all employees and eventually moving the plant to other places. The company has several plants in the state of Ohio, none of which are running at capacity, and at which there is excess capacity which would be sufficient to take care of all the production now being made at Latonia." The commissioners decided to defer Kiger's ordinance one week, effectively killing it.

At Kiger's third meeting on December 3, 1936, he made his first ever motion as an elected official to adopt the annexation ordinance, which was seconded by his emerging political ally, R.E. Culbertson. The motion was rejected 3-2. His first political item failed. Voting against the ordinance were Mayor H.A. Knollman and Commissioners William Beuttel and H.A. Meimann.

Robert Ed (R.E.) Culbertson was born in Falmouth, Kentucky and moved to Covington as a boy. Prior to elected office, he served as Assistant Director of the Covington Public Works Department. Over the next few years, the Kiger-Culbertson Coalition would be on the losing end of many votes. Together they would introduce many resolutions that went down to defeat by a margin of three to two. However, Kiger would slowly build a coalition that would eventually lead to a turning of the tables. The administration coalition was much stronger at this point than at any other in Covington history. Beuttel and Meimann were close friends as were their families. Meimann was the grandfather of future Kentucky Senator Richard Roeding who served Kenton and Boone counties for many years. He called his grandfather a 'gentle and jovial man who played it very straight." Later in life, he always carried Chuckles candy in his pocket and all the children knew. They would always get in his pockets. For years he served as president of the St. John's Orphanage, at a time when the board president did most of the work. When Meimann went to board meetings, Roeding would tag along and play with the kids while his grandfather worked. A soft spoken, stocky man, he always wore a hat, vest and suit. His grandson called him a civil politician, but one that was "not going to be turned around if he believed in something." Like so many Covington residents, Meimann eventually moved to the suburbs and is buried in the same cemetery as the Kigers.

Theodore Kluemper was born January 30, 1886 in Covington and, like Kiger, his early childhood influenced his sense of civic responsibility. His parents, J. Bernard and Maria Elizabeth Olges, immigrated like so many others to Covington from Germany. Bernard died young leaving Maria to raise Theodore on her own with three other children. At thirteen, he went to work at the Ibold Cigar Company in Cincinnati, rising over his thirty year career to superintendent. In 1908, he entered the political work of Covington by running for commissioner and receiving the third highest vote total of the twelve running. His service to Covington was wide and varied. He served as Council President, Chief of Police, Commissioner, Commissioner of Public Safety, and eventually City Manager. His 32 years of service saw the most important changes in governmental structure in Covington history. When originally elected he served under the council-ward form of government as Council President for three consecutive years. This was the longest tenure in Covington history. Like the famous political reforms across the river in Cincinnati, Covington also threw out the old boss political system. While no one as famous as Cincinnati's Boss Cox governed Covington, reform was necessary. In 1913, a charter system of a mayor and four commissioners was created and Kluemper was the first commissioner. He was re-elected again in 1915 and 1917.

Carol Elsner Rekow, in the <u>Northern Kentucky Encyclopedia</u>, describes an event that happened on March 5, 1918 as the highlight of his career. Upon entering a board meeting of the Ninth Ward Building Association for the annual election of officers, three men aimed guns at Kluemper and wanted money. According to Rekow, he stalled for time by going to his coat for his gun and kidded that "there is no money here." "Within seconds the men re-aimed and fired into the adjourning board room mortally wounding board members John Rehm, 82 and Andrew Nordmeyer, 67. Kluemper, now armed, shot and killed bandit Zeke Moran." Two other robbers fled, but based on Kluemper's identifications, were captured and eventually executed. Surprisingly, Kluemper lost his re-election bid in 1919, but won again in 1923 and served until 1929. During this time, he participated in another reform of city government as it switched to its present city manager form. However, Kluemper opposed the switch to the city manager form of government.[24] Across the river in Cincinnati, under the leadership of the Cincinnatus Association and Murray Seasongood, they made the same switch to this more professional form of government. In 1934, Kluemper was appointed as city manger by Mayor Joseph Pieper and the commission, putting him on a political collision course with Carl Kiger.

On December 10, 1936, following up on a campaign promise, Kiger seconded a motion by Culbertson encouraging the state to purchase the Suspension Bridge. Construction of the Roebling Suspension Bridge started in 1857 and after delays caused by the U.S. Civil War, opened to traffic in 1867. The specimen wire bridge was constructed prior to Roebling's Brooklyn Bridge and is one of the treasured historical landmarks of the region and the country. Making transportation free was a Kiger priority and the Culbertson-Kiger resolution followed up on newspaper reports that the State of Kentucky was going to buy the C & O Railroad Bridge. The resolution stated, "Newspapers report that efforts are begin made by the State Highway Department to purchase the C & O Bridge. We commend these efforts of the State Highway Department but would urge said State Highway Department and the Governor to purchase the Suspension Bridge also and at the same time."[25] The motion passed unanimously. Kiger had his first legislative success, all-be-it a simple resolution. However, it was one that helped work toward a campaign promise and toward a top priority of the newly elected commissioner. During this same meeting, an ordinance was proposed regulating traffic and movement of vehicles on public streets. Culbertson and Kiger moved the ordinance be referred to a committee of the whole. On Christmas Eve of 1936, the traffic ordinance dealing with bus routes, one-way streets, and penalties was passed by a vote of four to one. Kiger voted with the majority and Culbertson was the one dissenter. It was the first difference in vote for Culbertson and Kiger, even though Kiger's first commission meeting had only been twenty-five days earlier.

Kiger missed his next meeting on New Years Eve. Little did anyone know, but the approaching year of 1937 would mean disaster for the City of Covington and it was only a couple weeks away.

On January 14, 1937, the commission met and dealt with improvements to sidewalks and setting the tax rate for sidewalk improvements. It was the first time Kiger voted on a tax. Two days later, disaster struck. On January 16, 1937 the Ohio River crested at 51.66', just below flood stage. The chronology of the flood shows a dramatic rise in waters as compiled by the Kenton County Library:

January 16, 1937 – The Ohio River crested at 51.66' (flood stage was 52"). Weather Service predicts receding water.

January 17, 1937 – Heavy rains fall throughout the Greater Cincinnati area.

January 18, 1937 – River exceeds flood stage of 52'. Crest is predicted at 58'. Fourth Street Bridge between Covington and Newport is closed when river level reaches 54'.

January 19, 1937 – Ohio River rises to a level of 60'. In Covington, floodwaters cover Riverside Drive and block the Ludlow Street Car Line at the intersection of 3rd and Crescent Streets in Covington.

January 20, 1937 – Steady rain. Army trucks sent from the Fort Thomas Military Post to flooded districts in Northern Kentucky. Forty blocks in Newport are underwater.

January 21, 1937 – Ohio River reaches 63.1'. *Kentucky Post* headline reads, "River May Pass 66-Feet as Heavy Rains

Continue." Seventy-eight families in Covington have been forced from their homes, another 68 are on a waiting list. In Newport, 500 families have been forced to flee. Bromley in Kenton County and Silver Grove in Campbell County are completely cut off from neighboring cities. In Dayton, 35 city blocks are under water.

January 22, 1937 – Ohio River reaches 70.6'. All Greenline Streetcar service discontinued. The C&O Bridge between Covington and Cincinnati has been cut off due to high water. In Covington, many families are being housed in the Bavarian Brewery complex on Pike Street. African-American families are being housed in the Covington City Garage. Bishop Francis W. Howard opens all Catholic Churches in Covington for relief purposes.

January 23, 1937 – Snow falls in the Ohio Valley. Ohio River Reaches a height of 72.7' – the highest in recorded history at that time. The Covington Waterworks ceases pumping water. Waterworks superintendent reports that a 10 to 12 day supply of water is being stored in the city's reservoirs. Covington Schools Superintendent Glenn O. Swing orders Lincoln-Grant, 3rd and 6th Districts Schools closed. All three buildings' boiler rooms are flooded. Members of the American Legion are sworn-in at Covington as special deputies to assist in relief activities. Covington Fire and Police employees are working 12-hour days. This evening, three babies are born at St. Elizabeth Hospital without the benefit of electric lighting. Gas service is cut off in the City of Bromley and parts of the City of Ludlow.

January 25, 1937 – Black Sunday: 2.55" of rain fell in a 24-hour period. Ohio River is back on the rise. In Kenton County, over 30,000 citizens have been forced to flee their homes. Covington

Mayor H.A. Knollman declares a state of emergency in the city. He calls for the rationing of food, water and other supplies. All places of amusement as well as saloons are closed. The only southern means of exit from Covington is across 16th Street to Jefferson Avenue and out the Highland Pike to Fort Wright. Booth Hospital in Covington is housing 50 homeless persons despite being without heat. St. Elizabeth Hospital in Covington is housing 300 patients.

January 26, 1937 – Ohio River reaches a crest of 79.99'. Rationing continues and the National Guard arrives in Covington. Most of the region is left without electricity.

January 27, 1937 – Ohio River begins to recede. Flood damage in Northern Kentucky is estimated at $6 million. Covington Mayor Knollman requests the aid of 100 army personnel to assist in patrolling the city.

January 28, 1937 – Government officials urge citizens to be inoculated for typhoid.

Between 12,000 and 15,000 Northern Kentuckians were forced to leave their homes and transportation links between Covington and Cincinnati were flooded. Only the Suspension Bridge and the C & O Railway Bridge were usable. Martial Law was considered for Covington and, in order to cross the Suspension Bridge, permits were required. The bridge was to be used for food transportation and medical supplies. Water and electric supply was shut down. It was not until February 5, 1937 that the Ohio River was back within its banks.

On January 21, 1937, the city commission met and Culbertson and Kiger, moved and seconded, a motion urging Congressman Carl Vinson of Georgia and Kentucky Senators Barkley and Lodge to "exercise their good influence in receiving an appropriation of the Senate and Congress of the United States of America for the purpose of construction and maintaining a flood control dam on the Licking River near Falmouth." This motion passed unanimously. While this may not seem a priority during the first days after a disaster of this size, it was probably good politics. The need for the Falmouth Dam would not be more evident than during such an event. The construction of a dam in Falmouth has long been discussed and was the number one priority of Falmouth Mayor Max Goldberg, who served 33 years as mayor beginning in 1965. Goldberg died in 2007, living to see his city destroyed by the flood of 1997, but never to see the construction of the dam he championed. The Covington resolution by Culbertson and Kiger is one of the earliest actions regarding the construction of the dam as an important political issue.

At this January 21st commission meeting, the commissioners unanimously approved authorizing police and fire personnel to enter houses in the flooded district and report. It was added this would only be authorized during the present flood. They also voted to allow the city humane officer Tom Parker to use city funds for "flood sufferers."[26]

At a special meeting on January 26, 1937, the commission passed an ordinance affirming the previous declaration of emergency and authorizing the mayor to make all necessary orders and creation of penalties for violation. Kiger seconded this motion, which was made by Commissioner Meimann. A motion was made to build a pontoon bridge at Fifth Street east of Madison to Scott.

During this crisis, emergency ordinances and resolutions were passed authorizing a sinkhole repair at Ninth and Philadelphia, ironically by the location of Kiger's wife's childhood home; truck weight limits; and a resolution of appreciation to Troop F 123, Calvary Kentucky National

Guard. Resolution 6649 approved on February 11, 1937, expressed appreciation to many including the Latonia Refining Company for services during difficult circumstances.[27] Many ordinances were passed during this time, including for several years, those authorizing the demolition of framed buildings damaged during the flood. The first of these came in mid-February. Many years later, damaged houses were still scattered around Covington, many occupied. Jim Kiger recalls selling fruits and vegetables with his dad at houses on the site of the current IRS building. These houses were severely damaged by the flood, but fifteen years later occupied and in bad shape.

The teamwork evident during the immediate flood was soon to end. While the commission worked well together during the flood, passing ordinances and resolutions unanimously, other matters often saw disagreement.

The first came in February when Culbertson introduced a resolution, seconded by Kiger, to authorize the city to join as a plaintiff in a suit pending in Kenton Circuit Court. The case *Joseph Herbers v. the Cincinnati, Newport, and Covington Railway Company (CNCRC)* which is seeking to prevent said street car company from buying their bus lines in violation of the constitution of Kentucky and causing the public to be charged a sixty percent increase in fares."[28] The fear on Kiger and Culbertson's part is the company is attempting to control the bus lines in Covington. They felt this attempt to buy lines would increase fares 5-8 cents in going to Cincinnati from Covington and this was in violation of the Kentucky Constitution 201 "prohibiting a common carrier from buying competing lines of another common carrier which would lend to create a monopoly and prevent competition."[29] The motion was defeated by a vote of 3-2 with Beuttel, Meimann, and Mayor Knollmann voting against. On February 25, 1937, Ordinance 2951 fixing the salaries and compensation of agents and employees of the city for the fiscal year ending December 31, 1937 was voted on. Culbertson and Kiger wanted it laid over for a week. They lost this attempt three to two and Meimann and Beuttel motioned to pass the ordinance. It passed three to two.

In early March, the commission dealt with another flood issue when the Chamber of Commerce wanted them to enact legislation authorizing the execution of plans for the control of floods in the Ohio River Valley under the direction and supervision of the Army Corp. of Engineers. Like other flood legislation, the commission voted unanimously and in this case requested the resolution be sent to individuals including President Roosevelt, Senator Barkley, and Congressman Spence. Culbertson and Kiger sponsored this motion.

On March 10, 1937 the CNCRC issue surfaced again. Keeping in mind transportation and fares was a major platform issue with Kiger, he and Culbertson were trying a different approach after the failure of joining the lawsuit last meeting. Kiger and Culbertson wanted, as they say; "to give the citizens of Covington an opportunity to express themselves concerning the proposal now pending before the Council of Cincinnati." They believe the contract signed in 1917 between the City and CNCRC was for twenty-five years and the council was attempting to raise rates from 20 to 60 percent. The Kiger-Culbertson resolution stated, "Individuals are requested to live up to the letter of their contracts. Should not a public entity be required to do likewise? This means much to the working people of Northern Kentucky to have a five cent fare. The utility company signed the agreement in 1917 during war time. They should be required to carry it out unless the Council of Cincinnati sets aside the contract of 1917. Therefore now be it resolved by this mass meeting that the city officials of Covington protest officially against the unwarranted request by the CNCRC to the City Council of Cincinnati."

The resolution went on to say the commission appoint a committee of three, appointed by the chair, "to express the sentiment of the Citizens of Northern Kentucky in this unwarranted attempt by the CNCRC in trying to break a solemn and binding contract to the detriment of the traveling public.[30] The city solicitor advised against this motion. The motion failed three to two. It would seem the Kiger –Culbertson coalition was building toward a successful election campaign issue for the fall.

Twice in the last few weeks the administration had been on the side of fare increases for transportation to Cincinnati. Kiger, in a letter to the commission said, "Your vote on this ordinance will indicate whether or not you favor people paying an exorbitant charge for transportation that is entirely unreasonable. Let us not be fooled by some technical definition, but let us declare ourselves for five cent transportation which can be had if the C N & C Railway Company will permit us to operate the city in transportation matters."[31] At the March 18, 1937 commission meeting, Kiger and Culbertson tried again with their ordinance. It again failed. At this meeting, their coalition was also on the losing end of an ordinance, number 2952, lying and fixing the ad valorem tax at $1.29 per $100.00 of taxable property. In April, Kiger and Culbertson voted against the budget ordinance appropriating revenues and in May a plan was developed for transportation facilities to persons living in Rosedale and West Latonia by directing and authorizing the operation of busses over certain streets in the area. This would be subject to approval of the commission and the CNCRC. This action allows CNCRC to serve additional streets and widen James Street for buses. The administration ordinance 2976 says "changes of routes and substitution buses for electric cars" and the widening of James Street will be for the benefit of the city and the traveling public. Kiger and Culbertson tried to delay this action but were unsuccessful. It passed along coalition lines. Later in May, not giving up, Culbertson and Kiger would call for the repeal of 2976 which failed three to two. Petitions were presented, most likely instigated by the anti coalition faction, led by Kiger and Culbertson, opposing to street widening. It had no affect on attempts to repeal the ordinance.

In July, the commissioners did agree on one issue. The commissioners felt it was difficult to balance the city budget and one of the main reasons is the increasing cost of maintaining offices of county officials without charge to the county.[32] The only legal way to charge for the offices was for the county seat to be moved from Independence to Covington and this would have to be submitted to the voters. Unanimously, the commission directed the city manager to prepare a petition to get this question on the ballot. The motion was made by Kiger and seconded by Culbertson.

On July 11, 1937, new trolley cars were put into action on the Rosedale and Latonia Lines. As the new Greenline busses were dedicated, 200 invited guests watched. The Kentucky Post reported, "The ceremony started slightly before 11 a.m. when the Columbia System Band under the direction of Jake Hoffman began a concert. At 11:00 a.m. a fanfare from the band and a series of aerial explosions brought the dedication party to the band platform." In attendance, to celebrate this event, were Mayor Knollmann, Commissioners Beuttel, Culbertson, Kiger and Meimann, City Manager Kluemper, and City Solicitor Ralph Rich. Less than two months earlier, Kiger and Culbertson had voted no on commission actions leading to this celebration.

This ceremony was an important point in Covington transportation history. The Greenline Company began operation in 1887. Through the years it converted from horsepower to electric. Conversion to electric and expansion caused financial trouble for the Greenline and it was sold to the Cincinnati, Newport, and Covington Railway Company.

By the 1930s, the combustible engine had advanced and more roads were paved. The five-cent fare that Kiger opposed the elimination of was a tremendous burden to the railway company. As such, they began to convert to motor busses and trolley cars. The trolley cars still needed overhead electric lines, but ran on paved roads.[33]

---

[24] NK Encyclopedia, The University Press of Kentucky, 2009

[25] Resolution 6638

[26] Covington Minutes January 21, 1937

[27] Covington Minutes February 11, 1937

[28] Covington Minutes, February 1937

[29] Covington Minutes, February 1937

[30] Commission minutes, March 10, 1937

[31] Kiger letter to Commission March 16, 1937

[32] Covington Minutes July 15, 1937

[33] Northern Kentucky Encyclopedia, University of Kentucky Press, 2009

CHAPTER 4

THE ELECTION OF 1937

       Being summer time, thoughts started to turn to the fall election. The battle lines were drawn and the 3-2 split between the factions was pronounced. Which side would the voters support? The <u>Kentucky Post</u> would say this election "has resolved itself in to (sic) a contest of anti-administration candidates' verses the administration. The battle for ballots has produced no new issues. In fact, the campaign is being waged over the same ground on which the years' old struggle of a protesting minority in Covington has fought against the group in control"[34] While the newspaper took a neutral stand in this election, it did say City Manager Theodore Kluemper was an honest and faithful official. The anti-forces of Kiger, and particularly Culbertson, would make the city manager a major campaign issue. Many candidates would jump into the race.

       Former commissioner T.M. Swindler entered the race. He had served from 1930 to 1935 and was the founder of Swindler Funeral Home, a business that still thrives today. Swindler was the son of B.F. Swindler, the pastor of Madison Avenue Baptist Church and was himself a deacon at the Latonia Baptist Church. He married his first wife, Lula Rose, who was the daughter of Allison P. Rose, the founder of another funeral home, in 1910. She died young and Swindler later married his second wife, Viola. In 1935, he ran for mayor but was defeated by Knollman. In announcing his candidacy, he made only one pledge: "I will not buy the nomination or election, and if elected, I will not peddle or sell the power vested in me."[35] His grandson, Ed Currin, who still operates the funeral business, said his grandfather campaigned out of the garage behind the funeral home.[36]

Setting the tone for the campaign, R.E. Culbertson stated he was in favor of the current city manager retiring. In his announcement for re-election, Culbertson held nothing back. He seemed the angriest, but as an incumbent he had many specific points to make in favor of his re-election and in outlining his record. He covered a lot in his announcement statement.

William Good entered the race pledging a "new deal in the city government through his and the efforts of his associates on the anti-administration ticket, Culbertson, Kiger, and Swindler." Good, a businessman, had never held public office but in announcing his candidacy said, "With the City of Cincinnati setting an outstanding example under a charter form of government similar in many respects to our own, I cannot see why we cannot have good government."[37] This was clearly a shot across the bow of the administration and he added "on one side you have money, jobs, and promises; on the other, the offer of decent, independent administration." Good said he was proud to be on the ticket with the anti-administration faction, calling them men who have successfully proven to the City of Covington that they cannot be controlled. He announced the men he had aligned himself with had high standards, and he was confident they would "treat all businesses, private and corporate, just and alike." "If not," Good said, "I certainly would not align myself with them." Good also said he would, as an elected commissioner, let the city manager operate in a manner that was intended under the council-manger reform. This is an example where Good did not always sound like an anti-administration candidate. He did not always seem to believe the same things as Kiger.

Three candidates of the anti-faction were in the race, all with a consistent message of the administration being controlled, corrupt, and playing favorites.

Carl Kiger was in the race as well, bringing the anti-administration candidates to four. In his statement announcing his re-election campaign, Kiger said, "This year the voters of Covington will again choose between candidates backed by the utility forces and candidates who are openly opposed to control of our city by those forces." Kiger, at the beginning of the campaign, set the stage by saying, "I am and always will be opposed to operating the city for the benefit of public service corporations." Kiger outlined, as he announced his re-election bid, his accomplishment during the short time he had been a commissioner. His theme for re-election was clearly going to focus on the utility issues, but also his belief of introducing legislation that as he said, "are in the best interest of the greatest number of people." To him, this meant an honest civil service system, putting Covington on a "pay as you go" budget system, citing the fact Covington spent $75,000 more than budgeted in 1936, divorcing utilities and city government, and opposing negotiations by the city manger with, as he said, "a favored few." Repeating the common theme of Swindler, Good, and Culbertson, Kiger said, "I go into this campaign free and unshackled, having made no promise to deliver any favors in return for votes and as city commissioner will resent by my voice and vote any attempt political or otherwise to improperly influence my vote."

The stage was clearly set with the anti-administration coalition making influence peddling of the administration the central issue of the campaign. All the members of the coalition were on the same page. As individuals, they may have had some issues as a higher priority than the other coalition members such as the current city manager to Culbertson, utilities to Kiger, and good government to Swindler. However, they were together. Also, the issues raised by the coalition at the beginning of the campaign echoed those of the early days of Kiger's first term. He and

Culbertson advocated against higher transportation costs, for the state buying the C & O and Suspension Bridges, against budget and appropriation legislation, and in favor of annexation in parts of Latonia. They had set the administration up brilliantly, putting them on record for higher transportation costs and higher spending.

Exactly who was the leader of this anti-administration group? When Kiger came on commission, Culbertson had already been there. If there had been a coalition at the time, who was the leader? Was it Culbertson or Kiger? The two firebrand politicians had strong personalities. As the incumbent, many recognized Culbertson as the leader. However, the anti-administration coalition was more in a developing phase than anything. In 1936, Kiger ran as an individual. The anti-administration forces developed over the course of 1937 and by the election later that year, was a true coalition united against the administration. One year after Kiger's election, he and Culbertson had formed a tight political bond.

On Monday, October 11, 1937, Mayor Knollmann took the first shot at the anti-administration coalition. Speaking at Turner Hall, he specifically went after Commissioner Culbertson and his attacks on the city manager. He charged that Culbertson had "proposed to him a year ago that many city employees be removed and replaced by others and that City Manager Theodore Kluemper be replaced." The mayor said he wanted to "answer and refute" the statements made by candidates for commission as they made their announcements. In giving his remarks, Knollman periodically praised City Manager Kluemper while blasting Culbertson. He said, as reported in the Kentucky Post on October 12, 1937, "Mr. Culbertson charges that the City Manager and his group withheld matters pertaining to the City's government from the minority group. My answer to this is that for approximately a year, the entire

Board of Commissioners was called into caucus preceding every meeting to discuss pending matters. Later this was discontinued because the minority did not do likewise and more especially because we disapproved of it being first submitted to the 'Secret Cabinet' of the minority. Knollmann declared, 'you decide.' "Now you decide who were within correct procedure - those who consulted with the city manager to expedite the city's business or those who submitted their personal prerogatives to a 'Secret Cabinet'."[38]

Mayor Knollmann also hit Culbertson hard at handling of issues related to the flood. Reacting to the term "City Manager's Group," the mayor praised the volunteers who worked during the recent flood saying, "there never was a better or more efficient band in any crisis of human events." While clearly an overstatement, the mayor went on to say "the credit goes to them, not me." Referring to criticism levied by the anti-administration, the mayor said it was not possible to criticize their response without also criticizing the volunteers who did so much. At Turner Hall, the mayor introduced the rest of his administration candidates. Those running for commissioner were incumbent William Beuttel, Henry Meimann, and Frank Vaske. It seemed the mayor had hit a good theme. Was Culbertson criticizing the flood volunteers? It did not really matter if it was true, it was a good speech. Culbertson was placing some blame on the mayor for acting in a strong capacity. The mayor pointed out that Culbertson voted for the emergency ordinance giving the mayor certain powers as defined by Kentucky Revised Statutes including as the mayor would say, "complete control."

Commissioner Culbertson responded quickly. He accused the mayor of violating the spirit of the City Manager Act and "holding a club over the heads of city employees, in order that their loyalty in the present campaign will bring about a continuation of their reign". He sarcastically thanked the mayor for introducing Beuttel, Meimann, and Vaske as "administration candidates" proving his point that the commissioners are not individuals but rather a faction looking out for their best interests." Culbertson claimed city employees were going door to door collecting signatures on petitions for nomination of the Administration commissioner candidates. Once turned in, they were to distribute campaign literature. He cited the fact the mayor at the Turner Hall rally was introduced by city employee and tax collector, James McGarry. Culbertson accused McGarry of telling employees that "unless they got results, they would lose their jobs." Culbertson said this coercion of city employees would continue until after the election and is proof the city manager form of government is not being implemented the way it is supposed to be. In response to the caucus meetings, Culbertson countered that the mayor would call meetings just before the commissioners were to meet and did not want discussion on issues going before the board. He cited as the best example the ordinance regarding bus routes in Latonia. "They did not want any discussion of the bus franchise by the Men's Club of Latonia or any other group of interested citizens."

Culbertson also hit hard on the city's finances. He accused the city manager of ending 1936 by spending $76,000 more than the budget allowed and having a $176,000 in unpaid bills. He also cited that the current majority, over his objection, issued bonds to cover debts from 1934-1935, a time Kluemper was city manager.

Commission candidate Swindler campaigned and hit hard his theme of "the spoils system still being with us." He argued, "In reality we do not at this time have the city manager form of government, but the old spoils system in its ugliest form." He called it "disgusting" that city employees were working to elect the "utility ticket," as he cleverly called it, in order to save their jobs. Swindler told the voters that Culbertson, Kiger, and Good, will revive the city manager form of government and make it operate the way it was intended. In the greatest irony of it all, Swindler was quick to point out that Kluemper, as a commissioner, opposed the city manager form of government. "Does it not seem inconsistent that Mr. Kluemper should be placed in this very important place after being repudiated at the hands of the people for opposing the city manager form of government?" Swindler had a track record on commission to back up his theme of professional government. Swindler previously supported switching to the city manager form of government and was actively against the old spoils system. He was elected to the first charter commission after the cleaning out at City Hall. Not liking the implementation of the new system, he wanted back on commission to make it right.

In November 1929, the voters of Covington elected four individual businessmen who had promised to appoint a city manager. A gentleman by the name of Col. James Franklin was their choice as the first city manager. The candidates elected were Charles Zimmer, Sr. who defeated Theodore Kluemper by a vote total of 11,686 to 6,730; Louis Meyer who defeated Wm H. Newhall, 12,151 to 5,949; Joseph Pieper who defeated Thomas Bailey 12,151 to 5,949; and Swindler who bested John F. Kingsley 11,903 to 6,283. Zimmer was a hardware store owner, Meyer owned Louis Meyer Motor Company, Pieper operated a jewelry store at 616 Madison, and Swindler owned a funeral home. Each of these men promised to pay $3,000 out of their $3,600 salary for paying Bell's salary.[39] Kluemper was the most vocal critic of the city manager form and was strongly opposed to these four advocates. After the four businessmen were elected, Kluemper would sue the city to in an attempt to stop the switch to the city manager form of government.

It seems strange that the anti-administration coalition seemed so strongly in support of the city manager form of government. Kiger had been on record in favor of a strong commission. Perhaps the new form of government was becoming more accepted.

Albert Benjamin Chandler, better know as "Happy " Chandler, was born in 1898 and twice served as Governor of Kentucky, was a United States Senator, and Commissioner of Major League Baseball. He eventually would be elected to the Baseball Hall of Fame. Quite the character, Chandler earned his nickname because of his fun approach to life. In 1940, he challenged Kentucky Senator Alben Barkley, the Senate Majority Leader, and lost. Seemly this would be a disaster, but the affect on Chandler seemed limited. In fact, shortly after his loss he was appointed to the Senate following the death of Kentucky's Junior Senator, Marvell Mills Logan. Twenty years after his first term as governor, he was elected again after running on the slogan, "Be like your Pappy and vote for Happy." Defying political logic, the Chandler administration found itself mixed into the 1937 Covington commission election.

In fairness, Governor Chandler never took sides in the campaign, but his supporters did. Known as the Friends of the Frankfort administration, Theodore Hageman of Crescent Springs announced his friends would work for the election of the Covington administration. Hagemann, said the friends of the state administration, after careful consideration, "have decided to throw their weight behind the (Covington) Administration ticket." A controversy grew. Was it really possible for the Friends of the State Administration to separate themselves from Chandler? The only thing they all had in common was their support of the Chandler administration. It is generally not smart politics and provides no advantage for a state administration to get involved with a local primary campaign. The Kentucky Post editorialized,

"We cannot concur in the judgment of the local Chandler men in their support of the Covington Administration."[40] They added that while the Friends of the Frankfort Administration said the governor is taking no part in the election, "it will be difficult for the public mind to separate the chief from his lieutenants." Governor Chandler did hold a rally at the Covington City Building for other democrats already on the general election ballot. In response to a question at the rally regarding the Covington controversy, the governor said, "Leave me out." He quipped, "I don't even know who is running for Mayor. If I wanted to run Covington, I'd move up here and run for mayor. But I'm pretty busy down in Frankfort. Let me out of your municipal race."[41]

In all, twelve individuals were competing for the Covington commission in the primary of 1937. Only eight would advance to the general election. The October primary saw approximately 13,500 voters and as is typical, heavily favored the anti-administration and administration candidates. Candidates unaligned finished out of the running. William Beuttel finished on top with 6,605 votes. The final results were all close with only 1,526 votes separating the first and seventh place candidates. The results made it clear, the November election was between the anti- and administration forces:

Commissioner William Beuttel 6605

Commissioner Henry Meimann 6472

Commissioner Carl Kiger 6282

Frank Vaske 6152

Commissioner R.E. Culbertson 6064

T. M. Swindler 5701

William Good 5079

Louis Ante 1738

Meyer Siegel 1490

Edger Lemker 1089

James Higgins 719

L.L. Dawkins 633

The first seven to move on to the general election were all members of one of the coalitions. Louis Ante was the only independent candidate to move forward. Despite having one less candidate moving forward, the administration ticket immediately said they would not include Ante as a part of their ticket in November. Following the primary election, there was speculation that anti-administration voters voting for either Kiger or Culbertson were not as supportive of the other anti-candidates. In fact, it was possible voters in favor of Kiger were not always supportive of Culbertson.

Election Day results proved the speculation was true. Carl Kiger finished on top with 9,285 votes. He was the only anti-administration candidate to win. R.E. Culbertson finished fifth with 8,332 votes. Elected to the commission with Kiger were William Beuttel, 9,001, Henry Meimann 8,794, and Frank Vaske 8,654. Vaske would replace Culbertson putting the administration forces in a 4-1 majority. Across Kenton County, voters rejected removal of the county seat from Independence to Covington.

Carl Kiger was now the clear leader of the anti-administration coalition. However, he was not about to give up his goal of a City Hall takeover. The election of 1937 was clearly a major set back. Culbertson, the most vocal of the critics had lost his seat. He was out front for the anti-administration forces and it cost him his seat. The next two years would be frustrating for the anti-administration Commissioner Kiger, but they would live to see another day. Culbertson was not finished.

[34] KY Post, October 28, 1937

[35] KY Post, September 35, 1937

[36] Telephone Conversation January, 20, 2011

[37] KY Post, September 28, 1937

[38] Kentucky Post, October 12, 1937

[39] Kenton County Historic Society September, 1991

[40] KY Post, October 23, 1937

[41] KY Post, October 23, 1937

Covington City Building, c. June 1970

Crescent Street

1937 Flood

President Franklin Roosevelt, Kentucky Governor Happy Chandler, and Senator Alben Barkley leaving from train station in July 1938

President Roosevelt speaks in July 1938 in Covington, KY
(Photo courtesy of Kenton County Public Library)

Mayor Henry A. Knollman, the 20th mayor of Covington
(Photo courtesy of Kenton County Public Library)

R.E. Culbertson was at the side of Carl Kiger politically and professionally throughout Kiger's career

Covington Mayor William Beuttel, Jr. in his later years

The Rosegate House in Boone County, Kentucky. The summer home of the Kiger's and the site of Carl Kiger's murder
(Photo courtesy of Matt Becher)

Carl Kiger, political leader and, at age 49, murder victim

Carl Kiger's wife Jennie, son Joseph, and daughter Joan during the murder trial

CHAPTER 5

1938: DISAGREEMENTS CONTINUE

The split between the minority and majority coalitions on commission was clear from the time they took office in January 1938. The first action was to elect Beuttel vice mayor for a two-year term. Early on, Kiger was on the losing end of 4-1 votes to authorize the mayor to enter into an agreement with the City of Kenton Hills to provide fire protection, a city manager recommendation on the budget, the tax of 1.29 per $100 assessed value, ordinance 3028 appropriating revenue for the city, water rate increases, and a major fight related to a franchise agreement to provide gas. All of this was just through March. The administration had the power and the anti-administration coalition was at its weakest. At no point from the time of Kiger's first election in 1936 to the time of his murder was the coalition weaker. Most of the issues where there was disagreement between Kiger and the administration coalition were very public and controversial. The commission voted upon the recommendation of the city manager to increase the minimum water bill from eight dollars to $10 for the year. Kluemper said the tax rate would have to increase by 25 cents. The manager cited damage from the flood and increased maintenance and operational costs. All administration commissioners voted for this increase. Kiger voted no. The rate increase became effective immediately.

At the same time, the commissioners voted and passed the second reading of an ordinance selling a twenty-year gas franchise. It was a very contentious meeting. Many citizens present booed, yelled catcalls, and called the commissioners robbers.[42] Former state Senator John Murphy, City Manager Kluemper, and City Solicitor John Rich dominated the meeting prior to the vote. A recent court ruling required the Union

Light and Power Company (ULHPC) to give refunds owed to the citizens. Many present wanted the refunds distributed prior to any franchise agreement. Carl Kiger was the lone dissenter in granting the twenty-year franchise and he had several objections. He mostly was concerned the agreement gave the winning bid, certainly ULHPC, exclusive rights. Kiger said, "In its present form, the franchise would hamper any other company in laying pipes and lead to many suits and injunctions."[43] Kiger said, "This is just about the same as a perpetual contract." He wanted other things addressed including provisions for a discount if sub-standard gas is supplied, a specific site identified for a caloric meter to measure the content of the gas, and a provision allowing for changing some of the regulation of the agreement, because he felt it "had too many rules and regulations". Kiger felt there was no way to prove if ULHPC was making too much profit and going to the Public Service Commission with rate issues was cost prohibitive. Senator Murphy spoke and made the argument the refunds should come first and said the "city had been negligent in its fight to obtain the refunds."[44] Finally, a vote was called for and Kiger was the lone dissenter. The audience hissed and booed. Mayor Knollman shouted, "Thanks for the compliment."

Knollmann was furious, and administration commissioners would only get more upset as they were forced to backtrack on their vote. The Good Government League took immediate action. They circulated a petition with approximately 5,000 signatures on it to block the twenty-year franchise sale. The administration stayed defiant and said they would give it close scrutiny. Commissioner Meimann said, "We'll fine comb the petition."[45] Discussion took place regarding a six-year franchise, but the Good Government League was opposed to any agreement of more than two years. A second petition was simultaneously prepared. The mayor and commissioner refused to verify to the Kentucky Post a two-year agreement would be voted on. The petition against a six-year franchise was submitted with 9,036 signatures. The administration commissioners were coming around to the fact they had a problem. The League President, Albert Keller, said the "people of Covington are sore at the attitude of the City Commission."

The commission repealed the twenty-year ordinance and on March 24, 1938, voted in favor of a six-year franchise agreement. The motion passed 4-1 with Kiger again voting no. The Good Government League was successful in getting a referendum on the November ballot. On April 14, 1938, Polk Laffoon, Vice President of ULHPC, told the city they will stop selling gas to Covington and its residents on April 25. This, of course, was a legal formality. The city would then seek an injunction resulting in providing gas until the referendum was settled.

The main administration voice in defending the commissioners' twenty-year franchise vote was Assistant City Solicitor Rich. He issued statements and responses supporting the commissioners.

Despite political rhetoric during the previous winter's campaign, the commission seemed to vote unanimously on issues related to the 1937 flood. On June 2, 1938, Kiger made a motion authorizing the city manager to file an application with the U.S. Government through the Federal Emergency Administration of Public Works for a grant for improvements to the pump line of the Covington Water Works. A week later at the June 9, 1938 meeting, the Kenton County Fiscal Court agreed to pay the City $10,500 dollars in rent even through they occupy seven tenths of the City Building. The city manager said it was not enough and recommended rejection of the offer. Kiger was absent, but the remaining commissioners agreed with the manager. On the 28th of June, the commission discussed the Flood Control Act providing for construction of reservoirs in feeder streams to retard the flow of water, thus preventing heavy flood losses. The commission said the "Licking River has been a constant problem. The Licking River, they said, caused the "greatest portion of damage." The commission requested the federal government designate the project on the Licking River for immediate construction.

JACK MAYNARD

Jack Maynard was born in Pikeville, Kentucky on July 4, 1902. His father, Ira, was in the coal business. Jack attended Marshall College and the University of West Virginia, where he studied engineering. Following college, he worked for the Pike County Road Department, the State Highway Department, a private company, and the Appalachian Power Company. Eventually he went to work for the federal government and after one year was assigned to the Works Projects Administration (WPA) as a supervisor. In 1936, Jack Maynard, a man in his early 30s, moved to Covington following his transfer by the WPA. Weighing 200 pounds, Maynard stood at five feet and ten inches. In this new capacity, he became involved in city affairs including work in Devou Park and other recreational locations. Later in his career, Maynard would serve as the city manger in Wilson, N.C. from 1955 to 1969, when he was forced to resign because of bad health. During his career, Maynard served as President of the North Carolina City Managers' Association and was honored in 1968 for twenty-five years of service by the International City and County Management Association (ICMA). He served as Vice President of ICMA, the professional association of city managers.[46] His wife Anna said he was "a visionary civil engineer who always planned five years ahead." Maynard died on July 2, 1971 at the age of sixty-eight at the Wilson Memorial Hospital in Northern Carolina. He was buried in

Lexington, KY at Hillcrest Cemetery. Thirty-one years before his death, Maynard would get his first city manager position in Covington.

BARKLEY FOR SENATOR

The remainder of 1938 was relatively calm with attention focused on the election of a United States Senator. Carl Kiger was the Kenton County Campaign Chairman for Alben Barkley. In July of 1938, President Roosevelt would visit the Latonia neighborhood of Covington in support of Barkley. Kiger would play a major role in the event. Barkley's opponent was Kentucky Governor Happy Chandler. Barkley was a conservative democrat as was Kiger. Kiger's choice of Barkley over Chandler made sense. Chandler was a populist in the Huey Long tradition. Barkley was honest and a reformer, although, Chandler had many reforms as governor. There was no republican force in Kentucky then and elections were contested between democrats. Born in 1877 in a log cabin on his father's tobacco farm, Barkley rose to be Vice President of the United States. First elected in 1932, Barkley was clearly Kiger's most powerful political friend. At the time of the 1938 election, Barkley was the majority leader of the United States Senate. He would later become Truman's vice president after giving a tremendous speech at the 1948 Democratic Convention. After serving the Truman Administration, he would return to the Senate after beating the popular John Sherman Cooper. He died in 1956, one and a half years into the final term. Kiger found himself in July of 1938 making a major defense of Barkley after his opponent in the primary, Governor Happy Chandler said the Presidents' recent visit to Covington "was detrimental to Senator Barkley's cause and had lost him friends." Kiger was quick to point out the President's endorsement of Barkley. "I have no doubt that Governor Chandler would be a good senator from Kentucky, but I think Governor Chandler would be the first to acknowledge that as a junior member of the Senate that it would take him many, many years to match the national knowledge, the experience in the affairs of our nation, of that son of Kentucky, of whom the whole nation is proud—Senator Alben Barkley." Kiger lashed out at Chandler. He said, "Our beloved President need no defending from me, nor does Senator Barkley. Their records of accomplishments for the people of the nation and our beloved state are visible on every hand." In what can only be seen as Kiger sarcasm, he added, "The President has a nice, gentle and gentlemanly way of talking to Governor Chandler as a father would talk to his own, advising and imploring with him to listen to wise counsel, telling him that his inexperience in national affairs would be of little help to the state or nation compared to Mr. Barkley's long experience and ability." Again with the sarcasm, Kiger reflected, "When Chandler ran for governor he was elected by the people of Kentucky for four years and the people of Kentucky are expecting him to finish out that term and I am quite sure the people throughout Kentucky are going to see that he does." Kiger called Chandler running against Barkley, "ridiculous."[47]

Throughout the fall campaign, Kiger was focused on not much except the re-election of Barkley. Two rallies, one in Ludlow and one in Covington, were scheduled for July 27th. It was clear from the Barkley campaign they were going to stay close to the Roosevelt Administration and many accused them of trying to continue to hold onto his coattails. Barkley, in several speeches said not voting for him, was "a repudiation of the new deal."[48] However, Chandler was a loyal new dealer and the charges were false. Roosevelt was careful at the Latonia speech to speak kindly of Chandler. Historian Lowell Harrison, in the Northern Kentucky Encyclopedia, recalled how Chandler would board Roosevelt's whistle stop train tour in support of Barkley whenever possible and appear next

to the president.[49] Kiger said the July 27, 1938 Barkley rallies "will be an
old fashioned political meeting with a band, red fire, and all the
trimmings." At the time, the Ludlow rally began at the James Rigney
Stadium, a band started playing at the public square at Seventh and
Madison Avenue in Covington. They would play until Barkley arrived for
the Covington speech. Kiger, in promoting the event, said "we hope that
every Kenton County resident who can be present will be on hand at the
Wednesday night meetings. I know that this county, which has so
strongly supported President Roosevelt in every election since 1932, will
give the President's close friend and loyal defender one of the greatest
welcomes ever accorded a guest in this community." Both rallies were
successful. In Covington, Kiger introduced Senator Barkley. Cars had
been blocked from near the square starting at 6:00 p.m. and small
American flags were given to the crowd. Barkley hit Chandler hard with
many personal attacks including the disloyalty of Chandler running against
him. Barkley took credit for getting him elected governor. He quipped,
"But I did not know the damned fool was going to run against me."[50]

Barkley quickly returned to Northern Kentucky, and Kenton
County in particular, for three rallies at the close of the campaign. This
time, former governor A.O. Stanley would attend and announce support
for Barkley. Stanley was the 38th Governor of Kentucky, serving from
1915 to 1919, including during World War I. Prior to serving as
governor, Stanley served thirteen years in the United States Congress, and
after his term as governor, six years in the United States Senate. Historian
Lowell H. Harrison called Stanley's administration the apex of the
Progressive Era in Kentucky. Among the reforms adopted during his
tenure were a state antitrust law, a campaign finance reform law, and a
workman's compensation law.[51]

Kiger, in promoting the three rallies Barkley would do, said "Senator Barkley has been known throughout Kentucky, and particularly in Northern Kentucky, as an outstanding liberal".[52] Also appearing would be John Y. Brown. Brown was a Kentucky State Representative and served one term in the United States House of Representatives. His son John Y. Brown, Jr. would become governor of Kentucky in the 1980s. No longer holding political office, Brown would run for governor and lose the next year, in 1939. Kiger called Brown "a young man so well known to Kentuckians of all ages that I need not mention his record as a statesman and his ability as a speaker." Kiger called the Brown appearance, "the close of the local campaign for Barkley."[53]

Each local appearance by Barkley included heavy participation in, and support of, labor. The rallies had labor representatives proudly displayed up front and as speakers. Labor unions all over the county endorsed Barkley. As Election Day approached, Kiger said, "Kenton County will give Senator Barkley a majority. Just how large the majority will be, I will not attempt to say."[54] All told, however, a Barkley win in Kenton County would be considered an upset. Chandler was favored, mostly because he has always done well in northern Kentucky. The Chandler campaign expected to have a huge margin of victory in Northern Kentucky.

Kiger was right. Senator Barkley won Kenton County by approximately 700 votes, 9,960-9,206. Kiger issued a statement saying, "the upset victory of Senator Alben W. Barkley in Kenton County was attributed to Senator Barkley's record which attracted labor, the common people, friends of the new deal, and friends of President Roosevelt." He added, "We had a perfect organization and the loyalty of all the workers. You can't beat that."[55]

Kiger, basking in glory, had much more to say in his victory statement following the election:

"In a contest that engaged the attention of the people of this nation; one that all agreed was to be a test of the New Deal popularity, the common people decided in favor of Senator Barkley, leader of the New Deal forces in the Senate. Fundamental issues were involved in this contest that affected the lives of all our people. Allied against us were the forces of reaction, both within and without the State. They were attempting to retard the progress labor is making with the help of our President and Senator Barkley. When I accepted the chairmanship for Senator Barkley in Kenton County, I was mindful of the deep responsibility of that position. I was satisfied though, that if our people had the facts, they would decide wisely. This they did. The people of Kenton County can be particularly happy over the fine majority they gave Senator Barkley. In a county where the opposition expected a majority for their candidate of at least 5000 and where the greatest efforts were expended for the Governor, Senator Barkley triumphed. Our people in Kenton County can be assured that they have not only made Senator Barkley happy, but they have also gladdened the heart of our beloved President. No campaign Chairman had a more loyal or devoted group of helpers in any campaign. Their tireless efforts without any expectation of reward, is a tribute to their good citizenship and intelligence. I wish to thank everyone who helped in this great effort for common ideas and I invite the forces of Democracy to join me in a united march to victory for Senator Barkley in November."[56]

Kiger's statement was a mixed bag. In analyzing his statement, it is hard to imagine this was a very prudent statement in one big way. Following a primary victory, the goal of the winner is to re-unite the party for the general election. Instead, Kiger chose to take additional shots at the opposition, calling them forces of reaction. He did, however, strike other smart themes. The vote strongly indicated the New Deal was popular in Kenton County as was the President. Kiger championed both these themes. "We gladdened the heart of our beloved President," Kiger said, and he encouraged voters to carry this to a united victory in November.

CIVIL SERVICE REFORM

After working long days for two months, Kiger went on vacation later that week. Barkley went on to defeat Republican John P. Haswell by a margin of 62 to 38 percent in the general election. With Kiger on vacation, the city commission on August 11, 1938, adopted the first reading of a civil service ordinance creating a civil service board, examinations, and other components typical of a civil service system. This ordinance would amend previous ordinances related to civil service. The same month this first reading was adopted, a group of 140 applicants sued the city and the current Civil Service Board claiming the recent examinations for police and fire were unfair. They would win in court. In mid-September, the commission gave its final approval to the civil service reform ordinance. A public signing of the popular law was held with all commissioners and the city manager in attendance. In March, 1939, nineteen people would pass the new test, ending the controversy over the examinations.

THE BUDGET CRISIS OF 1938

The following month, Kiger and the other commissioners would differ on the issuances of bonds to help cover the city's debts. The plan was to issue $250,000 worth of city-funded bonds. The issue was placed on hold at the commission meeting in mid-September, pleasing Kiger. He felt, the city could "ease through this year without contracting additional debt". Kiger appeared to be correct in some regard. A spokesman for several holding houses, said the "bond market has the jitters". If you sell these bonds today, you will be disappointed at the price they bring. Final coupon rate will be lower than what Covington's waterworks revenue bonds brought."[57] On September 29th, the city commission voted to issue bonds in a first reading of Ordinance 3065. Carl Kiger was the lone no vote. On October 6th, the second and final reading was adopted with the same vote split.

It soon appeared both sides had been misinformed. The city had far more debt that the bond issue could cover or in Kiger's words, "to ease through the current fiscal year". The entire commission, including the administration members, and the city manager were about to have a major public disagreement. City Manager Kluemper announced the city had a debt of $532,344 - quite a sum for a city in the late 1930s. The commission felt misinformed and thought the bond issues were supposed to cover the city's debt. The manager blamed the commission. The commission blamed the manager. Kluemper said the commissioners knew the bond issues would not cover the entire debt, get all the financial information in their meeting reports, and authorized costs for projects not budgeted. Also, the city was still feeling the financial cost of the 1937 flood. A week later, the commission expressed its frustration with the manager. However, while the commission gave the manager a "stinging rebuke,"[58] according to the Kentucky Post, they also said no friction existed between the commission and the manager. Each commissioner signed a statement criticizing the manager, except Kiger. Kiger said he did not sign it because it was only shown to him immediately prior to the meeting.[59] Kluemper refused to take blame and proclaimed, "I can take criticism when it is coming to me, but I don't deserve this." He went so far as to say the commissioners are only in City Hall once a week and can't know what is going on. The commissioners in their signed statement took notice of this and said "the majority of the members of the board visit the City Hall daily" and all of us are at your beck and call by phone when needed or desire their presence."[60] Instead of doing his job by not publicly criticizing the commissioners, he was defiant. Kiger recommended the city manager itemize revenues and expenditures - a perfectly sound recommendation. Kluemper said he "would do absolutely nothing" about the recommendation.[61] Kiger called the monthly statements (September showed the city $60,000 under the budget) "jig-saw puzzles".[62]

Kluemper should have been fired because of his public criticism of the city commission. The administration commissioners saved his job. Kiger most certainly would have wanted him fired. At a special meeting on October 24th, the commission was told by the city manager, the city could not operate on a cash basis. The manager's point was that bills can't be discounted because the city will not be able to pay cash. Commissioner Kiger said "We ought to inform the people we buy from that we'll have to charge it." "You're taking the wrong attitude, Mr. Kiger," Vice Mayor Beuttel said. "We can pay, but not in time to get discount (sic)".[63]

FRANCHISE AGREEMENT RESURFACES

During late October, the gas franchise issue surfaced again. On November 8, 1938, a special election was held, allowing the voters the chance to repeal the six year franchise voted on by the commission on March 24th. The Good Government League, as the petition sponsor, and Mayor Knollmann campaigned on opposite sides of the issue. The vote of the citizens was to repeal the commission action. They did not like the six-year franchise. On November 25th, a new gas franchise proposal was introduced. It was for a two-year agreement and was to be put out to bid. It was unacceptable to Commissioner Kiger and the Good Government League. Kiger said it was the same as other proposals except in length. It did not contain the other demands of the Good Government League such as placement of a calorimeter, a discount in rates, and language on the gas refund. This first reading of the new franchise was approved 4-1, with of course, Kiger voting no. After his vote, Kiger said, "This franchise has so many objectionable features, that I can't begin to enumerate them."[64]

After first saying they were not going to fight this agreement, the Good Government League shifted their opinion and indicated they would fight this latest decision of the commission. Keller said signatures on a petition would be gathered in case a second reading is approved. Under Kentucky law, two readings are necessary for the commission to pass an ordinance. The commission's position was that they were following the will of the people. However, more than anything, the people wanted lower rates. This would carry into the election year of 1939. Besides the length of the agreement, the central fight still centered on refunds the citizens have never received. The former franchise agreement called for Cincinnati and Covington rates to be the same. Cincinnati's rate was lowered and rebates provided. Covington rates were also lowered, but no rebate checks were sent to its residents. Obtaining these rebates is why the city sued ULH&P Company. The city commission decided to again delay the two-year franchise and ask the Public Service Commission for a rate reduction. The decision was heralded by Kiger and the Good Government League.

Political factions, arguments, financial difficulties, a statewide election pitting an incumbent United States senator against a sitting governor, and other issues and controversies, dominated Covington politics in 1938. For Carl Kiger, the year could not have started out worse. His anti-administration coalition was reduced to only one member sitting on the commission. He was in the minority on many key votes and positions. However, as Chairman of the Barkley Kenton County Committee, he delivered a winning vote total, to the surprise of many, including Barkley. His stock with the United States Senate Majority Leader was very high. Also, and Kiger may not have seen it, but some of his stances and actions from 1938 were popular with the voters. He was doing well as the lone anti-administration commissioner. He was popular, liberal, strong-willed, and focused. The year 1939 would see more differences between Kiger, the mayor, and commissioners. As the year changed from 1938 to 1939, Kiger still had a long way to go toward reaching his dream. However, momentum and forces were coming together that might put his coalition in power in the elections eleven months away.

RELIEF FOR THE POOR CRISIS

A very large problem for the Covington City Commission surfaced in January of 1939. The Kenton County Fiscal Court cut off all of Covington's needy from their relief roles. This surprise announcement shocked the commission and the citizens. The county sent citizens seeking aid to the city manager who sent them back to the county. Kluemper was mad. Covington immediately cut off paying the county $2,910 annually for part of the salary for the head of the county office dealing with the poor and the $1,000 per month they give the county for relief. The president of the Good Government League could not resist the opportunity to take a shot at the city commission during this crisis. Keller issued a statement saying "we as citizens of Covington demand that you as the leaders of your respective governments call a conference immediately and bring about a solution.[65] He added, however, "we further wish to inform you that a committee of the Good Government League will confer with Judge John Northcut of the criminal division of Kenton Circuit Court in the hope that Judge Northcutt will see the need of impaneling a special grand jury for the purpose of investigation (sic) the relief set up and condition in the City of Covington." One can only hear the reaction the city manager and mayor must have had upon reading this letter. Arguments kept going back and forth between the city and the county. The city argued the county owed them money, including the rent money long a controversy. The county said 90 percent of the poor they provide service to, live in the city. The city manager began to provide some relief to the citizens with food and clothing. The mayor contemplated a department for the city to take over care for the poor.

After several weeks, the city and county came to a compromise, each agreeing to split the approximate $25,000 for providing relief to the poor in Covington. The discussions between the Covington commissioners and the fiscal court were long and hard. The meeting, at the old Kenton County Infirmary, saw the Covington commission working very well together. The city made an offer to pay $7,000 for relief. The county said no. The county countered for the city to pay $2,500 per month. The city said no, but offered to pay $10,500 per year, a major breakthrough. Commissioner Kiger played an important role, and when he asked for some figures to get to the bottom line on how much the city should spend on relief, things progressed further. The commissioners went to a separate room to discuss a proposal. The county computed the figures and both sides were back together. Many standing, the mayor called for everyone "to work harmoniously as we are all servants of the public." Commissioner Kiger urged, "We reach a solution of this problem now." Kiger presented the final proposals, based upon the new numbers, and both sides agreed.[66] The city added more money to cover half the salary of the county staff person in charge of relief programs. The disagreement between the county and the city for rent money was not discussed.

Albert Keller, at the same time the crisis with the county was going on, took a shot at the commission regarding parks in Rosedale and Latonia. The mayor said he heard from someone in the League that Keller was going to be a candidate for city commission and he surmised, this was the real reason for the calling on improvement to the parks. Keller pointed out the city commission in November had authorized $25,000 in order to get a $125,000 WPA project to build a band shelter in Devou Park, and other improvements, including a swimming pool near west Covington; and other structures like shelter houses and swimming pools in Rosedale and Latonia. In one of the great political retorts, the mayor, in discussing Keller's opposition to the West Covington swimming pool and his rumored run for commissioner, said, "this is well, but it is my belief that the public should be appraised of it for a better understanding of his motives so that when the star of Bethlehem again hovers and sets over Devou Park, the good people of Covington may know that to them a savior is born. And also that the well-to-do citizens of Park Hills may be warned that modern Pharaoh may again order a conscription so that the first born may not be permitted to use the swimming pool—not built for Devou Park."[67] Keller responded, "I will not be a candidate for city commission. Should I aspire for public office, I will do my own announcing."[68] In his equally humorous response, Keller said, "Your reply wandered over a period of 7,500 years and anyone who can distinguish a history book from a mail order catalogue knows there is no comparison between the Egyptian Kings (the Pharaohs) and your reign as mayor of Covington. History records that Egypt at the time of Abraham first entered it from the land of Canaan were more progressive than Covington the last three years, the period you have served as mayor. I would rather be remembered by monuments dedicated to the Pharaohs than to be a mayor of Covington and have as my only monument to prosperity my name inscribed upon a comfort station in a public park (Devou Park)."[69] Keller seemed zero for two in his political calculations for 1939.

CONTINUED STRIFE

In March, the franchise agreement issue was back in the headlines. The city administration commissioners decided to call for the sale of a ten-year franchise agreement. This new ordinance would eliminate the Cincinnati and refunds clauses from the current agreement. Why would the commissioners do this? It seemed like bad politics. However, the city commissioners met with a representative of the Public Service Commission. The representative, Hugh Bearden, informed the commissioners both of these clauses were contrary to the powers granted by State Law of the Public Service Commission. In response to a question from Commissioner Vaske on how a two-year agreement advocated by Kiger and the Good Government League would affect rates, he replied "services would be lessened because of a lack of interest on the part of bidders for a short, two-year agreement." Kiger correctly stated, "It is well understood that only one bidder, the Union, Light, Heat, and Power Company would bid." Kiger felt doing a two-year franchise would allow the city to put together a "real franchise" bid and that it would provide enough time to seek additional bidders.[70]

The commission approved the first reading of the ten-year franchise ordinance. Kiger, again, was the lone no vote. There was no real discussion and Kiger said he will outline his objections at the second reading. Neither the Cincinnati nor refund clauses were in the ordinance passed by first reading. The Good Government League threatened a large march on City Hall for the next commission meeting. John T. Murphy was so incensed, and said so are the people. He said, "10,000 strong will march on City Hall next Thursday".[71]

The commission decided to delay the second reading of the ten-year proposal until after the Public Service Commission decided on the rate issue. Keller continued to call for the commission to abandon the ten-year idea, even as it was put on hold. Mayor Knollmann said, "We are trying to strike a happy balance in the duration of the franchise, something that will please everybody concerned, but will not pass any franchise until we receive recommendations from the Public Service Commission."[72] By June, Kiger was in the headlines denouncing delays in the refund case.

As if enough was not happening in Covington to cause political strife, another issue surfaced in April. An organization existed in Covington called the Covington City Employees Mutual Society, a non-threatening organization of employees. They decided to discuss unionization and 150 members met on April 19, 1939 to hear from Frank Snyder an organizer of city, state, and county employees. It was reported eleven employees signed an application for a charter. The commission was surprised, thinking any employee issues were addressed by the civil service reforms. William E. Wehrman, a Kenton County attorney, served as counsel for the society and spoke on seniority rights. Straight time and vacation time had been previously addressed by the commission. Snyder, representing the Federation of State, County, and Municipal employees, said he would be attending a commission meeting to listen and afterward meet with the city manager. The eleven charter members met with the union representatives and called for 100 percent organization of city workers. The commissioners met with the employees along with Snyder. By then, 100 of the 300 city employees were rumored to have joined the union. Mayor Knollmann told the employees about the new civil service system and called it an "inviolable contract which can not be broke except by mutual consent of both employees and the City Commission of Civil Service."[73] He pointed out the city put employees of public works and water works on straight pay as requested, resulting in a $25,000 cost to the city. He asked them to figure out what they will gain by joining the union and discussed the city budget deficit. Showing just how different Kiger was from all the other commissioners, he spoke and said, "You have as much right to join the union as men working in trade shops." He continued, "For the city employees to join a union would work no hardship on the 'people of Covington' or the City of Covington." Joining a union will not make city employees "less efficient." "I don't believe it will be any more of a burden on the taxpayers than your present set-up."[74] The other commissioners, while acknowledging their right to join a union, encouraged better cooperation instead. A few months later, police employees created an organization called the Police Welfare Association.

In a small break in the administration coalition, Commissioner Vaske said the city was in a "rut" and needed "young blood" in city offices, meaning commission. He called for all meetings to be public, saying "by giving full publicity to meetings, we can get the best government." Vaske stated the obvious; the city was in bad financial shape and was using "out-dated methods." Hearing these comments, it would be easy to conclude Vaske was being a statesman and was going to step aside. Instead, he announced at the meeting he was running for re-election. No other commissioner would announce their intentions. This included Commissioner Beuttel rumored to be interested in seeking the office of mayor.[75]

On May 25, 1939 Kiger made a motion, passed unanimously, for all police cruisers to be equipped with sirens.

Finally, in July, the Circuit Court ordered ULH& P Company to pay Covington gas consumers at least $100,000 plus interest. The decision by Judge John Northcut revolved around the determination that refunds were retroactive and over the same time as refunds were made in Cincinnati.[76]

Throughout 1939, the budget continued to be a hot topic. By July, half the city departments were over budget. The mayor called for cuts in expenditures. While addressing various employees he indicated this could include cutting employees in the Public Works Department. He pointed out no one would be laid off because of union activity. The city manager was instructed to work things out with department heads and for them to live within their budget. Strains between the manager and the commission were still evident and mainly the result of the budget and financial issues. One example was over police car bids. One police car was delivered before the commission had approved of the expenditure.

JOHN Y. BROWN FOR GOVERNOR

In June, Kiger agreed to be the Kenton County Chair for the John Y. Brown Campaign for Kentucky Governor. This announcement was made after Senator Barkley endorsed Brown. Unlike the Barkley campaign, Kiger had a candidate nowhere near as good a campaigner. When Brown died in 1985, his son, the former governor, said "'my dad was naive in politics." He assumed the public would vote for him if he was the best man, which has little to do with it. And he would not organize the precincts, did not think that was the way politics was supposed to be."[77] Brown was running against incumbent Lieutenant Governor Keen Johnson. Johnson defeated Brown in the primary. Johnson actually became governor on the resignation of Happy Chandler on October 9, 1939, less than one month before being elected in his own right. Kiger had backed the wrong horse this time.

---

[42] KY Post, February 3, 1938

[43] KY Post, February 3, 1938

[44] KY Post, February 3, 1938

[45] KY Post March 31, 1938

[46] Wilson Daily Times July 30, 1983

[47] Kentucky Post July 15, 1938

[48] KY Post July 19, 1938

[49] Kentucky Encyclopedia, p. 179

[50] KY Post July 28, 1938

[51] NKY Encyclopedia, University of Kentucky Press, 2009

[52] KY Post July 29, 1938

[53] KY Post July 29, 1938

[54] KY Post August 5, 1938

[55] KY Post August 8, 1938

[56] KY Post August 8. 1938

[57] KY Post September 1938

[58] KY Post October 20, 1938

59 KY Post October 20, 1938

60 KY Post October 20, 1938

61 KY Post October 20, 1938

62 KY Post October 20, 1938

63 KY Post October 24, 1938

64 KY Post November 25, 1938

65 KY Post January 7, 1939

66 KY Post January 21, 1939

67 KY Post January 17, 1939

68 KY Post January 19, 1939

69 KY Post January 19, 1939

70 KY Post March 1, 1939

71 KY Post March, 1939

72 KY Post March 7, 1939

73 KY Post April, 1939

74 KY Post April, 1939

75 KY Post June 1, 1939

76 KY Post July 17, 1939

77 New York Times June 17, 1985

CHAPTER 6

<u>1939 ELECTION</u>

Election time came quickly. Candidate announcements at this point in Covington history would come late and not before September. The first to announce was Good Government League President Albert Keller. In announcing, he took the first shot of the political campaign and it was aimed at the city manager. "I favor the selection of a city manager under obligation to no group or political machine." He pointed out the inefficiencies he saw of the manager and cited as the best example, the budget problems and surprises. Ahead of his time, he proposed commission meetings be held at night. Addressing his favorite and best political issue, Keller said, "I have given many days of hard work in helping to hold back the ever-increasing power of utilities."[78] A couple days later, Commissioner Beuttel announced his candidacy for mayor. Kiger also announced for re-election to commission. Beuttel, in announcing, pointed out the commission has been able to get jobs for the unemployed and has kept taxes low. Taxes have risen in most cities since 1932, he said, but in Covington, they are four cents cheaper. He proudly mentioned the excellent water filtration plant and called it "second to none." He also called the new second line to supply water to their reservoir, a major accomplishment. Citing his four years on the commission, Beuttel said he has "the experience and knowledge to serve the people of Covington as Mayor."[79]

Kiger, likewise, announced he was running on his record. "My candidacy is based squarely upon my record while in public office. I am proud of my vote on civil service reform and, if properly administered eliminates political dominance and dictation. I will do everything in my power to see that this civil service is properly administered."[80] Again,

Kiger mentioned his strong belief utilities and city government must be divorced and no one company should have preference over another. "I go into this campaign free and unshackled making no promises to deliver any favors in return for votes. I will resent by voice and vote any attempt, politically or otherwise, to improperly influence my vote."[81]

The anti-administration ticket opened their headquarters at 4th and Scott streets. A rally attended by 250 people was held soon afterwards at the headquarters. At the rally they advocated for a properly administered civil service system, the right for city workers to unionize and for weekly paychecks for city workers. They also "avowed they were not obligated to any group or special interest."[82]

Other candidates jumped in. Mayor Knollmann announced for city commission. Former commissioner and county sheriff, Louis Vogt of 613 Pike Street announced, as did R.E. Culbertson. Others included: Nat Rogers, a café and restaurant owner; incumbent Commissioners Vaske and Meimann; William Harris, a member of the Health Board and owner of Harris Sales Company; Charles Brewsaugh, a foreman at Wadsworth Electric Company; W.S. Good; and Clarence Heitzman. In total, fifteen individuals announced for commission.

Culbertson, perhaps toning down his rhetoric from the last campaign, focused on his record of supporting the new filtration plant, the modernization of the fire department, his attempts to start a hospital, and advocacy of civil service. Commissioner Vaske made it clear he was "proud to have been a member of the administration that has been able to lower taxes and at the same time provide employment through useful public works."[83]

The administration ticket comprised of Meimann, Vaske, Knollmann, and Harris. Beuttel was their mayoral candidate. The anti-administration ticket included Kiger, Culbertson, Kenney, and for mayor, Cassidy.

In addition to Keller and Commissioner Beuttel, Ed Cassidy and John Murphy filed for mayor. Two other citizens entered also, R.S. "Doc" Payne and John J. Thobe.

The most interesting component of the race was the disbandment of the Good Government League and the resignation of Keller as president. The organization was now known as the Covington Civic Club and R.C. Stagman became the new president. According to the resolution adopted by the 25 members present, the League had "ceased to carry out the functions for which it was organized." It went on to say, "some of the Leagues officers have used certain tactics which have been repulsive to the public in general." The statement was directed at Keller.[84]

The Kentucky Times Star pointed out in an editorial that a lack of new industries was a serious problem and many candidates were running on a platform to do something about it. They asked voters to look at qualifications of candidates and "municipalities the size of Covington (and Newport) are pretty large corporations in which millions are spent in the course of a year and the money involved is that of the taxpayers."[85]

Turnout on primary Election Day was small. Beuttel and Murphy won the primary for mayor and would face off in the general election. The anti-administration ticket had lost its mayoral candidate. Beuttel won 3,633 to 2,923. Keller finished dead last behind two other lesser known candidates with 397 votes. Cassidy finished almost 700 votes behind Murphy. Keller was done as a political force in Covington.

In the commissioner race, Kiger finished first again in a blow out. Kiger again proved he was the most popular official in Covington. He most likely could have been elected mayor if he ran. In mixed results, Culbertson finished second, clearly getting support from Kiger voters.

The next three to move on in the field of eight were all administration candidates: Vaske (3,903), Harris (3,884), Meimann (3,720), and Knollmann (3,651). Kenney finished seventh and Vogt eighth.

The general election for commissioner two weeks away would provide clear choices between the two political factions. For mayor, Beuttel seemed the favorite. In fact, Kiger disavowed Murphy. One Kiger supporter said "our candidate for mayor was defeated."[86] The administration forces would put a lot of effort and resources to defeating Murphy and support their candidate for mayor. The administration ticket announced John Walsh a civic leader and manager of the concerts in Devou Park would manage the administration campaign.[87] Walsh said, "I believe it to be a civic responsibility of the highest order for our citizens to rally to the cause of good government when that good government is threatened by individuals whose unjustified attacks on men and policies is concrete evidence of their own lack of fairness and ability to serve the people."[88] Presenting, as he saw it, the excellent record of the administration was Walsh's goal. Knollmann said it is easy to criticize those in public office but "the proof is in the pudding.[89] Most important to the citizens are taxes and the administration has cut the tax rate from $1.33 per 100 valuation to $1.29. Knollmann said he is confident the voters will look at the record in casting their votes.[90]

The hardest hits on the campaign trail came from Beuttel in campaigning for mayor. Murphy, who was disbarred as an attorney, provided good fodder for Beuttel. Calling the office of mayor the "highest gift," Beuttel referenced Murphy's disbarment and an indictment in Hamilton County, Ohio. However, in fairness to Beuttel, he said Murphy's public record is what people should look at. When Murphy was elected state senator, he promised to vote against a sales tax. Beuttel said, "Look at Senate Journal for April 21, 1936, page 165. You'll find the same Senator Murphy voted for the 3 percent tax on your electric and water, which you are still paying today. The next day, Senator Murphy voted for the income tax."[91]

Beuttel also hit hard at the anti-administration commissioner candidates. Speaking at the Homeowners Administration Club Number 8 at the home of their president, Charles S. Moore at 31 W. 30th Street, he accused Culbertson of being anti-union, and asked why Kiger was "unable to understand the city's monthly financial statements."[92] Aiming straight at Kiger, Beuttel said, "Mr. Kiger raises the old bogy-boo about this being a fight against the utilities. That is a familiar cry in Covington elections. Mr. Kiger never has told you how he is going to secure lower rates when, as he well knows, the rates that are charged by all utilities in the State of Kentucky are absolutely under the control of the Public Service Commission of Kentucky. Mr. Kiger has not once during this campaign pointed out to the public just what constructive program he has in mind or what he intends to do. In all the time that Mr. Kiger has served as a member of the Board of Commissioners, not once did he offer a constructive resolution. On most public issues he voted 'no' not from understanding of the matter, but rather political effect."

Although not mentioned by the anti or administration tickets, this election would clearly decide whether the city manager would stay or go. The anti-administration ticket has been widely critical of Kluemper and their election almost certainly would result in his termination. The opposite would be true of the administration ticket, even though 1939 was a stressful time between the manager and the commissioners. They had supported the manager during a time when many would have fired him. Unions backed the administration ticket including the Brotherhood of Railroad Trainmen and the Allied Building Trades Council. The Kentucky Post also endorsed the administration ticket. The Kentucky

<u>Post</u> said the election of the administration ticket is a continuation of good government and referenced the accomplishments of the last two years.[93]

Candidate Vogt dropped out of the race and gave his support to the administration ticket. At this late date, however, his name would still appear on the ballot.

Election Day came on November 7, 1939. The election would set the direction for several years to come. Would the citizens give an overwhelming endorsement to one of the tickets or split the commission? A unique radio appeal was broadcast across Covington on election morning. "I'm Carl Kiger. I'm Ed Culbertson. I'm Marvin Keeney." This last minute radio appeal was very unique for a local election. They became known from this appeal as the "Three Musketeers," as they called themselves.[94]

For mayor, Beuttel defeated Murphy 9,734 votes to 6,684. The administration ticket, although not a surprise, kept the mayor's seat with Beuttel's election. This victory would prove to be one of two for the administration ticket.

The Kiger anti-administration ticket was swept to victory. Kiger finished on top with 9,734 votes, followed by Culbertson with 8,523, and Keeney with 7,963. The forth and final slot went to Harris, the only administration candidate elected to commission. The incumbent commissioners finished last and in the following order: Vaske (6,743); Knollmann (6,259); and Meimann (6,138). Vogt, having dropped out, came in eighth (1,434). The biggest surprise was probably the strength of Keeney and Harris, both newcomers.

City Hall had seen a revolution. Carl Kiger, a popular, strong labor, New Deal Democrat with a love and tract record of opposition politics, was its leader. Along with the new mayor, he would need to learn to govern. He had the control, the power, and the votes to do as he wanted. One of the first questions asked of Kiger's election night was about employee positions. Kiger answered, "If it means wholesale firing of city employees, the answer is no." The three commissioners must meet. This was not a good sign of leadership, as Kiger had already dismissed Harris as participating in future talks concerning key employees. Would the men in key positions keep their jobs, including the city manager? "We believe that they know whether they should resign and we feel that they will," Kiger said.[95] Of course, other employees were in civil service and protected. The key positions for the majority to appoint were the manager, solicitor and public works director. Kiger said change is coming. The ticket ran on change and the election gave them the power. Kiger said he thought the city manager would resign and would have done so even if the administration ticket had won. "A change means change in city managers," Kiger said. "Knowing he must now lead a government," Kiger said, "Greater responsibility comes with the majority as opposed to being a 'lone anti' commissioner." Again, forgetting Harris, "The people of Covington have placed the city's affairs in the hands of we three. That is a great responsibility."[96]

Carl Kiger had reached his dream and was now the leader of the Covington City Commission and possibly stronger than the mayor-elect. He had received approximately 1,900 more votes for commissioner than Beuttel did for mayor. In less than two months, his ticket would be the majority.

---

[78] KY Post September 26, 1939

[79] KY Post October 2, 1939

[80] KY Post October 2, 1939

[81] KY Post October 2, 1939

[82] Kentucky Times Star, October 1939

[83] KY Post October 5, 1939

[84] KY Post October 4, 1939

[85] KY Times Star October 1939

[86] KY Post October 24, 1939

[87] KY Post October 25, 1939

[88] KY Post October 24, 1939

[89] KY Post October 26, 1939

[90] KY Post October 26, 1939

[91] KY Post October 27, 1939

[92] KY Post November 3, 1939

[93] KY Post November 1, 1939

[94] KY Post October 31, 1941

[95] KY Post November 8, 1939

[96] KY Post November 8, 1939

CHAPTER 7

THE NEW MAJORITY

Anxious to get started, the new majority of Kiger, Culbertson, and Keeney, called a special meeting on New Year's Day, 1940. It started at 9:30 a.m.; just nine and a half hours after their term began. The first action was to approve a motion by Culbertson, seconded by Keeney, to elect Kiger vice-mayor of Covington. The vote passed unanimously. The next action, to go into executive session to discuss the city manager, was approved. Upon coming back out, a motion was made by Culbertson, seconded by Kiger, to suspend Kluemper as city manager. The motion passed 3-2, along coalition lines. The new majority had wasted no time in moving forward with the beginning of major change at City Hall. In his place, 37 year old Jack Maynard was selected.

The commission charged Kluemper with 12 charges of inefficiency and political activity. A hearing would begin in a few weeks. Maynard inherited a city with a debt of between $500,000 and $600,000. Debt would have to be brought under control. The new majority started out 1940, when the weather was as cold as ever. On January 5, the temperature was ten below.

Since the election, Covington employees had been nervous about their positions and the new civil service system. Maynard spoke to the employees. "Those who have been good workers should have no fear. I have always expected a day's work from those who worked for me and I will expect the same here."[97] He added, "We are going to stay within our budget, and be businesslike." Upon entering his office for the first time as city manager, Maynard found many flowers from well wishers. He immediately sent them to local hospitals and the Kenton County Infirmary.

The commission disagreed, 3-2 on appointments to the Board of Equalization, but agreed to appoint a Board of Inquiry, to "make a complete investigation of city financial affairs."[98]

In the first meeting of the new commission, the top employee was removed and replaced and appointments to one of the most powerful boards made. This trend of personnel changes would come to dominate Covington politics in 1940. The anti-administration coalition campaigned on change and they would deliver. However, it would not be without controversy. At the same time, the nation was entering World War II. The nation or the world would never be the same.

In just the first 15 days of 1940, the commission would meet six times. Many of their first actions dealt with the city's finances. They even borrowed money to use for payroll for the first half of January. Acting City Manager Maynard and Commissioners Kiger, Culbertson, and Keeney announced their support to hire a delinquent tax collector at a salary of $2,500 per year. The mayor and Commissioner Harris, preferred the current system of paying the collector a percentage. The current tax collector, Martin Brown, resigned, but mostly because he would be representing Kluemper at his hearing beginning on January 23, 1940. For the most part, all the commissioners were on the same page about the debt and the need to address the situation.

A new city solicitor, Stanley Chrisman, was hired replacing administration supporter Rich. The hard working Chrisman graduated from the University of Cincinnati Law School after working during the day and attending school at night. Working in the two-person Covington solicitor's office would require him to work just as hard over the next few years. Maynard requested, and received, the resignation of the Director of the Public Works Department, Ben Vastine. This came as no surprise as Vastine was another big supporter of the administration ticket. Two weeks into this term, police civil service exams became an issue again with a group of officers wanting them declared void. The new solicitor told the commission they had no jurisdiction or authority to set aside the exams.

For now, Maynard seemed satisfied with the performance of the police department and its chief. Police Chief Alfred Schid reported the police department came in under budget for 1939 and submitted ideas for improving operations. However, strife among police department employees was very bad. The department seemed factionalized and morale very low. Maynard would have to address this situation.

On January 18, 1940, Commissioner Kiger made a motion that was supported unanimously granting permission to the United Spanish War Veterans to conduct their annual carnation day sale on Saturday May 4, 1940.[99]

Aside from personnel issues, one of the biggest controversies of the new year centered around Mayor Beuttel's nominations to the Housing Board. According to the mayor, he was informed by the Covington Legal Department the Board of the Housing Corporation was not appointed in accordance with the law. Not more than two members may be of one political party. Kiger took the offensive. One democrat resigned from the board and one democrat changed his registration to republican. Kiger felt the mayor could only appoint someone to replace E.A. Cassidy, the democrat whom resigned. The Covington commissioners rejected the mayor's appointments several times and the mayor considered the current board illegal. Kiger led the commission to adopt a resolution authorizing a letter be sent to the U.S. Housing Administration supporting the current board. The resolution was passed 3-2, with the mayor and Commissioner Harris opposing. Kiger's letter, said, "the city commissioners are entirely satisfied with the present

members of the Covington Municipal Housing Commission Board and if
there was any doubt as to the eligibility of the members of the Board, or
any member of this Board, this doubt was removed when Linus Hand
changed his political affiliation. We have confidence in all the present
members of the Board and insist upon completing these projects."[100] The
federal government eventually said they would not get involved, it was a
local matter. The issue would go to the courts. The mayor would
eventually have to settle on this political issue.

In early February, Maynard Henry Jenisch, Covington Industrial
Director, and Charles O. Davis, assistant superintendent of distribution,
resigned from their positions. Maynard told Jenisch, "you haven't' been
doing the job."

THE KLUEMPER HEARING

Tuesday January 23, 1940, saw the beginning of the hearing on
the removal of City Manager Kluemper. It was expected the hearing
would take one week, involve approximately 15 witnesses, and the
introduction of many audits and records.[101] In all, twelve charges were
levied at the city manager and the outcome was pre-determined. It was
clear the majority members of the commission whom suspended
Kluemper would vote to uphold the decision. Mayor Beuttel and Harris
would vote to retain. Kiger, Culbertson, and Kenney would win this one.
The courtroom of Judge Rodney Bryson in the city building was packed.
Martin Brown, Kluemper's attorney, denied the charges except one. The
one exception was the suspended manager had, in fact, lent a city truck to
an employee for a short time after he requested its use. Throughout the
hearing, Brown went through each charge. Requests for dismissing
charges died because of a lack of a second. Solicitor Chrisman served, in
essence, as prosecutor. The hearing dominated the local news and was

often contentious and showed the factions of Kiger, Culbertson, and Kenney verses Beuttel and Harris on full display.

Kiger and his other two majority commissioners had done their homework. The period between the election and inauguration was dominated by plans to remove the city manager. This was goal number one. All other changes they wanted to make as the new majority would be implemented by the new manager. The twelve charges were so carefully written and in such detail, they took up most of four pages of the Kentucky Post. They went as far back as 1937 in their charges. Kiger, Culbertson, and Keeney, each signed the document they created leveling the charges.

The commission voted March 2, 1940, to make Maynard the official city manager, removing the title "acting."

PERSONNEL AND BUDGET ISSUES DOMINATE

The remainder of 1940 would be described as painful as the new majority continued to make personnel changes at City Hall and deal with the ramifications. On Friday, March 1, 1940, Maynard announced seventeen dismissals including some jobs that were eliminated. On March 1, Maynard said the city has "lived like the Joneses and must raise taxes to pay for the "spree."[102] Expenses must be trimmed and revenues must be raised. Refinancing bonds is necessary. Since 1927, he said, the city has issued $1,240,000 in debt and today the debt left is still $1,112,000. An employee-city commission meeting was called. The labor unions wanted it to be only between their members and the commission. Maynard said all employees would be invited. A couple weeks later, the commission voted 3-0 to adopt a salary ordinance and other conditions that satisfied employees and the unions. Beuttel and Harris decided to not vote at all in protest to it also including "higher bracket salaries."[103] In total the city was in debt to the tune of $3,734,000.

In late March, the commission had no choice but to raise taxes. The city tax rate was increased $.29 per $100 valuation. The majority members blamed it on the past commission. Beuttel said he voted against the increase because it was opposite his campaign pledge and Harris said the necessary revenue could be raised through collection of delinquent taxes. Harris said he would rather take a salary cut.

Continuing to cut, City Manager Maynard announced in mid-April thirty people would be removed from the payroll in the public works and water departments. In the days before the announcement some employees went on strike. Frank Crolley, a Covington city employee, sued saying he was discharged by Maynard without regard to his seniority rights. His attorney, J Richard Udry, filed two other suits, based upon different grounds. Judge Daniel Goodenough of the Kenton Circuit court agreed with Crolley. The court said, "It appears to us that the city manager has taken unto himself power and rights which are not delegated to him by the civil service act. Under the civil service ordinance, this plaintiff has certain rights. A mere change of the name and classification of the office should not deprive this plaintiff of his rights." Seniority rights begin at the time of employment, not at the time of adoption of the civil service ordinance, as Maynard had claimed. The city appealed. On June 21, 1940, the Court of Appeals agreed with Goodenough's decision. This decision was the first following the civil service legislation passed by the Kentucky General Assembly in 1939.   In mid-September, Goodenough would order three employees reinstated with back pay.

In February, the citizens won the gas rebate issue and could now expect to receive the money. The city won the rent case against the county.

On the financial front, a mixed report was presented to the manager and commission by comptroller Holman. Expenditures for the first five months were under budget by $33,683.64, but revenues were also under by $38,496.02. However, revenues were anticipated to meet projections by the end of the year. After six months the city would be under budget by almost $21,000.

The unions felt this savings came at their expense. They charged favoritism and disregard of seniority rights on the part of City Manager Maynard. The manager said in defending his actions, "The current administration of the civil service ordinance in Covington is guided only by economy and efficiency."[104] Clearly, the new civil service system of Covington was going through some growing pains and Maynard would be criticized by the courts and some employees reinstated. Charges of replacing employees with political appointees were leveled.

Closing out the year, Maynard shook up the Covington Health Department and removed the director.

REMOVE MAYNARD

By August, a petition was circulated to remove Maynard as city manager. The petition, created by the Covington Voters League, went so far as to require disgraced, disbarred and losing mayoral candidate John T. Murphy be named as the new manager. As the petition was presented to the commission, calling the manager unfamiliar with the city's problems and blaming him for the tax increase, Maynard chuckled to himself.[105] Kiger, leading the meeting as acting mayor in Beuttel's absence, referred the matter to legal counsel for an opinion. At the next meeting, the commissioners would reject the petition 3-0 with Beuttel and Harris refusing to vote. The League also presented a petition to abolish the City Manager Form of Government. It went nowhere.

By October, Maynard would revamp the police department. In early August, Commissioner Kiger's mother died and the commission adopted resolution 6926 expressing their symphony for the loss. The resolution signed by Mayor Beuttel said in part, "we offer to Carl Kiger our sincerest sympathy in the loss of his mother. The inadequate words of sympathy which we try to convey fall short of the feeling which goes out to our brother Commissioner in this time of sorrow."[106]

The year 1940 saw the new majority on Covington Commission focus almost entirely on internal operations of the city. Starting with the January 1, 1940 appointment of Maynard, changes kept coming. For better or worse, City Hall was much different at the end of 1940 than at the beginning. Kiger's first year in the majority had brought significant change to the daily operations of the city. There certainly were growing pains including unhappy employees and labor unions, entranced politicians, and the citizens wondering how this would all play out. The focus on internal operations by Kiger, Culbertson, and Keeney did not seem like smart politics nor was it something the general citizenry would care about. However, across many parts of the region and the nation, the decades preceding were ones of local good-government reform. The changes of 1940 in Covington were in many ways a continued growth toward ultimately achieving these reforms. Achieving the City Manager Form of Government is more than simply creating an ordinance establishing the position. Like any new system, change is incremental and evolves. The year 1940 saw dramatic progress toward achieving the kind of success earlier visionaries saw for the City Manager Form of Government and the City of Covington. Perhaps the biggest success of this first year of the new coalition is they took the position of city manager to a new level in Covington. This change can still be felt today as Covington now has a long history of a professional city manager. As a new year approached, many people recognized this dramatic change and were supportive. Some people, formally opposed to the Kiger coalition, now saw real progress. Others, however, continued to fight.

---

[97] KY Post January 2, 1040

[98] Covington Minutes, January 1, 1949

[99] Covington Minutes January 18, 1940

[100] Commission minutes January 25, 1940

[101] KY Post January 22, 1940

[102] KY Post March 1, 1940

[103] KY Post March 14, 1940

[104] KY Post July 18, 1949

[105] KY Post August 8, 1940

[106] Covington Commission Minutes October 10, 1940

CHAPTER 8

THE SECOND YEAR OF THE KIGER COALITION

At the beginning of 1941, the commission and Maynard were recognized and praised. It had been one year since the City Hall take over by Kiger, Culbertson, and Keeney and the ouster of City Manager Kluemper. Immediately, Maynard said, "a business administration is what we are going to have and we are going to stay within our budget."[107] On January 3, 1941, the Kentucky Post named Maynard the "Man of the Week". In doing so, the Kentucky Post said Maynard had "adhered strictly to budgetary limitations, has reduced the personnel, has moved toward an efficient health department, and will give greater service for every tax dollar. It is no secret that Jack Maynard and the new city regime have made real progress in bringing order out of confusion in City affairs."[108] The Kentucky Post had changed their mind about the Kiger coalition.

While the budget was now under some control and indebtedness had been greatly reduced, Maynard was rebuked in several court cases saying he dismissed employees with civil service protection. Some were eventually reinstated with back pay. However, with the $525,000 debt eliminated, the city budget balanced, some infrastructure improvements made, and employees having received raises, the city commission could now possibly consider lowering the tax rate. Generally, the citizens took well the increase of 1940 after seeing the tremendous financial mess the city was in. The city manager, on March 13, 1941 issued a report to the commission explaining the accomplishments of 1940 and recommending a $.10 decrease in the tax rate. He also presented the new budget.

The remainder of 1941 would continue these administrative accomplishments and expand some of the services the city could provide.

Investments were made in police and fire equipment, employees were given raises, and the budget remained balanced. By July, the cash balance would be up $81,641 dollars for the first six months of the year. Other issues would arise throughout 1941, but the most important was continued progress toward a stable budget and resolving personnel and operational issues. The growing pains of civil service administration continued to be an issue and the commission adopted some amendments to the Civil Service System in 1941.

---

[107] KY Post January 3, 1941

[108] KY Post January 3, 1941

CHAPTER 9

1941 ELECTION

      With all the success and progress, it was still anyone's guess as to how the electorate would respond. Generally speaking, the citizens seemed very happy with the progress and accomplishments of the new majority on the commission. Albert Keller continued his strong criticism of the new administration and he filed to run for commission. The other filings came including Culbertson, Keeney, and Kiger. The three struck a prior theme outlining the terrible financial mess the city was in just two years earlier. They pledged to continue to operate the city efficiently. Kiger took the lead in making their case. All three commissioners called their reforms "pay as you go". The city would have the money to pay their bills or would not incur the expense. Kiger said, "These policies have been strictly adhered to from the time I took office on January 1, 1940, until the present time and will continue as long as I remain your city commissioner. In addition, the past practices of borrowing money to take care of bond maturities and interest has been discontinued. This new administration is now placing the necessary money in sinking fund accounts to meet these obligations when they become due. When the present administration took over control, it was a recognized fact that the financial affairs of the City of Covington were in a serious condition. I desire to call to your attention the obstacles which faced the new board when it took over."

      "The city had a floating indebtedness of some $527,000; the payment on bond issues including both principle and interest in the sum of $76,000 was unpaid; the last half of the city employees

payroll for December 1939 amounting to
$26,000 was unpaid; there were unpaid
judgments against the city for damage suits
which had been taken to the Court of Appeals
and affirmed in the amount of $15,500; a note to
the city depository for $60,000 was also unpaid
all of which should have been paid in the year
1939. These obligations were paid by the
present city administration out of 1940 revenue.
This was positively verified when the report of
the certified public accountant, Cecil Hall,
disclosed that the city in addition to its
indebtedness, owed some $527,000 in unpaid
bills. The improvement in the financial
condition of the city today is amply reflected by
the fact that the city was able to sell bonds at an
interest rate of 2 ¼ percent. This improvement
is attributed to the pay-as-you go policy, the
setting aside of money in sinking funds to take
care of interest and maturities when they
become due, and the determination of this
administration to maintain the operations of the
city on a strict business basis. Monthly financial
statements now are submitted and have been
published in the newspapers".[109]

Talking about his own candidacy, Kiger said:

"Since I have been your City Commissioner, I have reached my decision on all matters which have come before the Board, after due and careful deliberation, and guided by my best judgment, advocated those things which I thought were for the best interest of the greatest number of people and I shall continue to vote for measures which in my opinion are for the best interest of the city of Covington and its citizens. I do not believe any one company should have preference over any other but all who are able to furnish adequate service should have an equal chance to bid and the lowest possible rates and the best franchises should be obtained for the citizens of Covington. I have always been mindful of the fact that the duties of a City Commissioner are a big responsibility and that a Commissioner is confronted with many problems for on Election Day he is chosen by the people as their special representative, and he must have the courage and convictions to represent them without fear or favor. While I shall solicit votes from all citizens of Covington to support me for City Commissioner, I go into this campaign free of political domination by anyone, making no promises to deliver any favors in return for votes. As City Commissioner, I will resent by voice and vote, any attempt politically or otherwise to improperly influence my vote. I submit these

policies as my pledge toward continued good
government and ask the citizens of Covington to
support me for re-election as City
Commissioner."[110]

The <u>Kentucky Post</u> endorsed the entire ticket and said "the record
of improvement in municipal government in Covington during the last
two years speaks eloquently of the reasons why voters should have no
hesitancy about electing the present City Commission."[111] They
specifically spoke of the elimination of $527,000 of debt, running
government more like a business, implementing an effective purchasing
system, expanding the health department, and beginning a project to
eliminate odor at Banklick Creek.

The voters spoke overwhelming on the record of the coalition of
Kiger, Culbertson, and Keeney. Kiger lead the voting, finishing well
ahead of the pack. Culbertson finished second, Keeney third, and Harris
fourth. Mayor Beuttel was not up for re-election. Kiger's coalition said
following the release of the vote totals, "the Kiger, Culbertson, and
Keeney organization considers it a mandate to perpetuate the efficient
pay-as-you-go, budget balancing policy which has been in effect for the
last two years. The majority commissioners pledge themselves to
complete the Banklick sewer project and to plan a program of
improvement for the city of Covington throughout the next two years."[112]
Albert Keller, never getting the message, finished dead last and far behind
even the next lowest candidate. Vice Mayor Carl Kiger, the most popular
elected official in the City had won his last election. He would be dead
before the end of his new term.

THE NEW TERM

Carl Kiger was nominated by Culbertson to again serve as vice-mayor. He was reappointed by the commission. With the war still raging, the commission passed a resolution allowing employees to serve their country without losing seniority. The commission also changed the Equalization Board, reappointing their friend and supporter E.A. Cassidy to another term, with all other members being first-time appointees. The year was relatively quiet for Covington, and by the end of 1942 the city had maintained its pay-as-you-go system. After all, this had been the main campaign pledge in the last election when the coalition was retained by overwhelming margins. Revenues were lower in 1942, but the budget remained balanced, deposits were made to the sinking funds, the waterworks department was making a profit, and other operations seemed to be doing well.

The biggest problem in 1942 was the brewing storm of employee salaries. The employees wanted more money, revenues were projected to go down again in 1943, and taxes might need to be increased. Working together, and putting their differences aside, the entire commission passed a budget raising the tax rate $.12 cent per $100 evaluation, with nine cents of it for the city and three for the school system. Harris, usually the odd man out, said, "While I object to increasing anybody's taxes at the present time, I know that the city employees deserve wage increases in view of the increased cost of living."[113] Recognizing he was going against his no tax increase pledge, he said if there was anywhere else to get it, he would. The plan gave employees a ten dollar a month raise with a total payroll increase for the year of $48,000. Vice-mayor Kiger said, I think we have the pledge of the entire board that if our income is less than the budget, we will live within our income." Kiger added he did not believe there had been a year in the past where all the commissioners entered into the work of cutting and cutting the budget as they have this year.[114] While the pay raise issues would eventually be settled, employees were not happy with the proposed raise amount. They threatened to strike but later voted not to walk out.

In the last few months he served as vice-mayor and a commissioner for the City of Covington, Carl Kiger made or seconded many motions. He made motions approving a $300,000 financial note; authorizing $500 for the apprehension and conviction of the person or person guilty of the recent slaying a resident; and a resolution on the death of the Mayor's wife. He seconded motions on the death of former mayor Daniel O'Donovan who served from 1924-1928; and another on the death of former Fire Chief William McAvey. These resolutions were routine and ironically often dealt with the death of someone connected to the city.

---

[109] KY Post October 7, 1941

[110] KY Post October 7, 1941

[111] KY Post October 28, 1941

[112] KY Post November 5, 1941

[113] KY Post March 4, 1943

[114] KY Post March 4, 1943

CHAPTER 10

<u>THE LAST TWO WEEKS</u>

While Vice-Mayor Carl Kiger had less than two weeks to live, there was one major political issue left for him to fight. Albert Keller, President of the Voter's League, sent a letter to Mayor Beuttel, calling for the removal of Carl Kiger. The mayor read it at the August 5, 1943 commission meeting. This would be Kiger's next to last meeting and the final one with any official action. It took place in Courtroom 108, the Common Law and Equity Division of the Circuit Court. It began at 9:30 a.m. in the morning.

Keller, through the letter, said Kiger should be ousted on the grounds he is a resident of Boone County and owns a farm in this rural section of Northern Kentucky. Keller said the "citizens resent the fact that Mr. Kiger, a resident of Boone County" should continue to mix in the "political and government affairs of the City of Covington." "We contend that Mr. Kiger's political interest is in the affairs of Boone County and not in the affairs of Covington, and that Mr. Kiger should devote his interest in Boone County affairs and let the citizens of Covington conduct their own political affairs." He went on to say that "Mr. Kiger's maintenance of his former residence on Crescent Avenue is a mere blind to enable him to continue to meddle in our political affairs and that he should be ousted from public office by members of the honorable Board of Commissioners." Keller says he bears no animosity toward Kiger and the League endorsed him when he was a resident of Covington.[115]

While no one knew it, the timing of this ouster move was both ironic and unfortunate. Keller was again embarrassing himself. The law was clearly on Kiger's side. At the meeting, testimony was even given pointing out the League doesn't really even exist as an organization. It was really just Keller.

Following the mayor's reading of the letter, Kiger spoke. "Inasmuch as the letter is about me, I would like to make a few remarks. First of all, I thought everyone, or almost everyone, knew that I had a summer home in the country. I want you to come out to it, and if you do come, I am asking that you do so before the snow flies, because I will be back in Covington before that time." "While this was not a great defense," he continued, "I have been receiving a lot of telephone calls from people telling me that if I don't do certain things they are going to tell that I have a farm. Where are we living? I thought this was a free country and we don't have those kinds of things here." Kiger then hit the League stating "I am just wondering what the Voters League is. The past few years we have been hearing a lot of talk about the Voters League. We see things in the paper about this and that (what) the Voters League says. This commission and the public should know who the Voters League is." He asked if anyone present "knows anything about the Voter's League."[116] Maynard said he had received several letters on stationary of the League listing 1418 Greenup Street as their address.

Responding to a citizen claiming the League does not exist, Kiger said, "I think the people are tired of this misrepresentation."[117] The commission filed the letter and it never became an issue. Other business included Kiger seconding a motion closing a 16.57 foot of alley on the north side of 19th Street. The last commission meeting Kiger ever attended took place August 12, 1943.

Five days later, Jennie and Carl Kiger celebrated their 24th wedding anniversary at their Rosegate home with an elaborate and fun party. The couple went to bed around 10:00 p.m. according to Mrs. Kiger. Shortly after midnight, 15 shots rang out hitting Carl seven times,

Jerry three times and Jennie once in the thigh. She faked death, saving her life. The three .38 caliber guns were owned by Kiger. During the trial of Joan Kiger, Dr. William McKee testified Kiger was shot from a distance of 18 inches and the killer "pumped bullets into Mr. Kiger". McKee was a Cincinnati Police pathologist.

In a controversy debated today, City Manager Maynard arrived , some describe, as minutes after the murder and took Joan into a room for 30-40 minutes. Speculation grew that he knew what happened and was protecting and briefing Joan.

FOLLOWING THE MURDER

On August 20, 1943, Joan attended the funeral of Carl and Jerry Kiger at 9:00 a.m. at St. Aloysius. The Solemn Requiem High Mass was sung, followed by prayers at St. John's Cemetery. The arrangements were handled by Middendorf Funeral Home. Following the graveyard prayers, a celebration was held in the annex of St. Aloysius.

The bullets that killed Carl Kiger also stopped a political career. It was widely rumored Kiger would run for mayor in the fall election. His murder had a profound affect on Covington politics. Immediately his coalition was tied with the opposition at 2-2.

The first regularly scheduled meeting of the commission following the murders was canceled out of respect for the vice-mayor. The first meeting of the commission following the murders, took place on August 26, 1943. Only routine business was conducted, including the rejection of a bid from Hatfield Coal Company to supply the city with coal during the winter. A resolution honoring the life of Carl Kiger was unanimously passed. Culbertson made the motion for adoption and Harris, made the second. It was recognized as in bad taste to bring up the issue of a successor at this meeting and it was never done. Doing so not only would have been disrespectful, it would have ignited a political firestorm. The new split on the Commission was Culbertson and Keeney; and Beuttel and Harris. The meeting was quiet and respectful. The resolution honoring Kiger read as follows:

> **Whereas,** the Heavenly Father has taken from the official family of the City of Covington, its vice mayor, Carl Kiger, and
>
> **Whereas,** we who have known Mr. Kiger for years now look back across the span of his life. He was born and reared in the west end of the city he served as vice-mayor. In his young manhood he was ambitious, never satisfied to plod along the path that others tread. He had aspirations to be a leader in his city. His thoughts, his desires, were to champion the cause of the poor and the working class of his community. His zeal in their behalf elected him a City Commissioner in 1937 and again in 1938, 1940, and 1942, and
>
> **Whereas,** we who have sat with him in council chamber have always found him looking after the welfare of the city. He was always zealous to see that the taxpayer's money was spent judiciously and wisely and that they received for each dollar spent, 100% in return. He fulfilled his office without fear or favor to anyone. His greatest desire at all times was to see that the right thing was done which would render the

most good to the people of this city. When he arrived at that time in his own mind his friends' entreaties or his enemies' threats could not swerve him from the path he had chosen to tread, and

Whereas, Mr. Kiger's life was centered in his family which he cherished above all other things, as their welfare and happiness was always foremost in his thoughts and his every effort was directed toward that purpose, now therefore,

Be it resolved by the Board of Commissioners of the City of Covington Kentucky: That in the death of Carl Kiger the city has lost an official who during his entire term of office strove to carry out the wish and the will of the people whom he served. That the Commission has lost a member whose counsel and advice they respected in their administration of governmental affairs. That the people of the City of Covington have lost the real champion of their cause whose place only time can fill. That his wife and family have lost a husband and father whose place can never be filled. To them in their hour of grief we extend our deepest symphony, realizing how little it will compensate for their tragic loss.

Be it further resolved, that a page in the City Commissioners' Minute Book be set aside and this resolution be inscribed thereon and that a

copy of said resolution be sent to the family of

Carl Kiger.

While not discussed during the immediate grieving period, a political question existed: Who would be the next vice-mayor, replacing Kiger? In very early September, just a couple weeks following the murders, Commissioner Keeney made the motion to appoint Culbertson vice-mayor. Culbertson immediately seconded his own nomination. In a surprise move, when the roll call reached Mayor Beuttel, he said, "in voting, I want to make a few remarks." He said Culbertson received the highest number of votes, except for Kiger, in the last election. He went on to say, he was voting for him in recognition of Mr. Culbertson's long service on the City Commission and because I owe a vote to Mr. Culbertson for a favor he did for me in 1936."[118] The final vote was 3-1; Culbertson succeeded Kiger as vice-mayor. Commissioner Harris was the lone no vote. The favor is lost to history.

---

[115] KY Post August 5, 1943

[116] KY Post August 5, 1943

[117] KY Post August 5, 1943

[118] KY Post September 3, 1943

CONCLUSION

In so many ways, Covington was a smaller version of the cities of New York, Chicago, Boston and even Cincinnati just across the Ohio River. It was influenced by the mob. Covington, Newport, Kenton County, and Campbell County finally were able to fight off these influences. It was after the time of Carl Kiger. The gaming, horses, and prostitution rings were eventually busted. For years, however, Covington was influenced by these corrupt forces and many of the politicians of the Kiger era must have known what was going on. Did they all take bribes? No. However, some did. Just ask the question, why did the police not break up the bars? According to Asa Rouse, most times "the State Police would raid the bars, the slot machines were hidden. The syndicate was tipped off, allegedly by the Covington Police."

Rumors abounded about the death of Carl Kiger who surely would have been the next mayor of Covington. He might have gone further. Some people claim it was a mob hit. Jennie would shut all the windows and lock all the doors at Rosegate, despite being in a very rural safe area. Jim Kiger thinks she might have been afraid of the mob, thus indicating Carl was not influenced by them. Joan's attorney, Sawyer Smith, said Carl "was obsessed with the idea of robbery and slept with a gun under his pillow." Is it a coincidence, Keller called for Kiger's removal shortly before his murder? It was nothing but a coincidence. However, general wisdom seems to dictate that Kiger, like many, may have been on the take. There was approximately $1,500 found in Rosegate at the time of the murder, stuffed in a couch. He had around $60 in his pocketbook. The rumors about the money abound to this day. Was it mob money? In 2011 dollars, $1,500 equals $18,700. Asa Rouse says the idea Kiger was murdered by the mob is "preposterous and doesn't bear comment." He is right. Carl and Jerry were killed by Joan, suffering from night terrors. The <u>Kentucky Post</u> called it a nightmare complex. Smith said "I do not mean just little nightmares, but horrible dreams defined by doctors as profound sleep lapping over into apparent wakefulness."[119]

Throughout part of this time frame there was a restaurant/bar located by City Hall. It was called the City Hall Café. Jim Kiger quotes a well-respected Northern Kentucky business person discussing the café. City leaders would meet there before council meetings. They would hear from contractors and others. The mayor would sit on one end, the commissioners around the table. Plates would be in front of each person. Contractors would place money under each plate. If it was gone from a majority of the commissioner's plates, they had the votes. "Keep in mind this was a time when Kiger made maybe $500 a year," according to Jim Kiger. While the $500 is most likely a low estimate, there is little doubt Kiger made much more money as a result of something. As Jim Kiger said, "It was a time when politicians not on the take would not get elected." Asa Rouse, believes the same thing. "It was wide open," Rouse said. "The rank and file citizens were not affected by the corruption." In Rouse's mind, "this was the world Kiger lived in. It was all so accepted and rampant. This doesn't mean Kiger was a bad guy." Rouse attended Dixie Heights High School and his classes had a lot of children of syndicate members. Rouse said, "They were the nicest kids; popular and honest. They kept their young family separate from the reality of the way the syndicate lived."

Bruce Ferguson shares this same belief. Ferguson, a man who has studied the murder extensively, believes Rosegate was purchased with syndicate money. Hush money was prevalent for police payoffs. He even questions if the $1,500 was hush money and Kiger was a distributor of the funds. Ferguson asks the obvious question, if no one was being paid hush money, why was gambling so "wide in the open"? Asa Rouse doesn't buy it. "The $1,500 was inconsequential," he says. At the time people often kept money out of the banks and making deposits were more burdensome in a time when banks were not on every corner. Like Ferguson, Rouse believes Rosegate was bought with money taken from the Cleveland Syndicate. Even during the immediate aftermath of the murder an investigation of "a pay off" by certain gambling interests of the $1,500 was conducted by the Boone County and Covington Police Departments.[120] The day before the Cincinnati Times-Star reported "it had been rumored about Covington City Hall that an anonymous caller had informed (Covington Police Chief) Schild that he had overheard three men in Ft. Mitchell discussing a "pay off" the night before Kiger and his son were shot to death."[121]

Regardless of these issues, how should Carl Kiger be judged? Clearly Kiger was an excellent politician. He had a short political career, but was able to quickly put together a coalition of individuals against the administration of the City of Covington. He was the coalition leader from day one. Eventually rising to vice mayor, his future was bright. At this time in Covington history, the vice-mayor had political power. If not for his murder, where would he have wound up? Certainly, he would have eventually been mayor. He had the connections and political savvy to go further.

Kiger was always consistent in his political statements; calling himself an independent, owing himself to no one, a fighter of the taxpayer, and the guardian against the utilities---and in the end he was. His votes on these issues were consistent and in line with what he said throughout his political career. However, as Jim Kiger said, he was no reformer. An opponent to the City Manager Form of Government, he believed in the old system and in the administrative and legislative powers of the commissioners. Having commissioners not involved in the day to day operations of the city was a crazy idea to him. After all, he was elected. However, when given control of the commission, he installed a more professional manager, one eventually honored by the International City and County Management Association for over 25 years of service. Kiger did give out jobs like the best of them. Jim Kiger's own dad got his job from Carl in the water department during the depression. Jim says, "If word came down that Carl wanted someone to have a job, they got it." Perhaps his greatest political achievement was leading efforts to fix the terrible financial situation in which the city found itself in the late 1930's and early 1940's. Also, being elected just before the 1937 flood was no piece of cake to manage. The city did its best. He advocated for civil service, ironically while giving out jobs.

There is no doubt Carl Kiger's greatest legacy is as the victim in the most famous murder trial in Northern Kentucky history. The trial was known across the country. In the back room of the courthouse during the trial, a telegraph machine would send news of the day's events across the country. Even as vice-mayor in such historic times, he would have been forgotten if not for the tragedy at Rosegate. Such is the funny thing called fate.

Mayor Beuttel never had children and died on June 22, 1973. He lingered toward death for a long time including internal problems since December and from a stroke he suffered in March. According to Virginia Gridley, "It was long rumored he may have been influenced by the Syndicate but there is no real evidence to prove this. It would not be a surprise if he was."[122] Gridley says she was given very expensive gifts by Beuttel such has a real electric stove and a doll from France. He drove a new LaSalle during the Great Depression. Of course, he was a very successful businessman. Gridley recalls Uncle William getting three cousins, including her, a job at City Hall typing and selling driver's licenses. He served as mayor through 1943 and eventually retired from his plumbing business. He also was President and Director of second Federal Savings and Loan Association of Covington. In 1922, a <u>Kentucky Post</u> reporter asked him what counsel he would give a young man starting in life. He answered, "Be honest and upright in all your dealings."[123]

Jennie Kiger lived another 37 years after the murders. Jim Kiger recalls her attending church every Sunday at Mother of God in Covington. She always sat on the right side in the back with several other older ladies. They all lived in the Panorama Apartments, a building for seniors just down the street. Jennie and the other ladies would always stay another 15 minutes after mass to pray. For years she worked at the old Coppins department store in Covington. Jim describes her as a very nice, quiet lady who would always say thank you. She lived her life with a limp from the shooting. The family would tell the kids it was from polio. Jim Kiger remembers as a kid when at Christmas all the children were running around playing and being loud. One child had a toy cap gun. He ran over to Jennie sitting in a chair, points the gun at her and shoots the gun at her. The loud room switches to dead silence. The boy is whisked away. Jennie died in June, 1979 in Oxford, Mississippi while living with her son after becoming ill. Her funeral mass was held there. A custodian at St. John's cemetery has recalled the story about receiving a call from an undertaker about digging the grave for Jennie. A hearse with two men pulled up after driving from Mississippi. He had three other men at the cemetery. They pulled the casket out and immediately placed it into the grave. No family, no church members, and no relatives were there. No prayers. She was just put straight in the ground.

Joan Kiger died April 5, 1991 at the age of 63 in Louisville, Kentucky. She moved to Louisville and obtained her degree from the University of Louisville. Changing her name to Marie J. Kiler, rumors had it she never married fearing the night terrors could cause something tragic to happen again. She had a successful career as a teacher. A few years ago, a group of citizens in Boone County put on a community play about the Kiger murders. A group of Joan's fellow teachers attended one performance and were shocked at her history. They had no idea. Jennie Kiger would secretly take a bus from the old Greyhound Terminal at 5th and Madison in Covington to Louisville. She knew where Joan was and visited often. Jim Kiger said rumors abounded on where she was going and people wondered were Joan had ended up. Most thought she moved across country, not just 100 miles down the road. Joan died in a nursing home and donated her body to the University.

Kiger's closest political ally, R.E. Culbertson was a good friend. He eventually became mayor and served from 1946-1948. He died at age 81 on June 20, 1960 and is buried in Highland Cemetery in Ft. Mitchell, Kentucky. He moved to south Ft. Mitchell and his visitation included a service by the Indra Consistory, Scottish Rite.

The simple marker at St. John's Cemetery hides the story of the tragedy of the Kiger family, especially the two murder victims. Carl was a bright and ambitious politician and Jerry, an innocent boy. Much has been said of the murders. Plays have been written and performed, books and essays prepared, and presentations made. None touch on the political career of Carl Kiger. By today's standards, many politicians of Kiger's day may have been thrown out of office and indicted for corruption. At the time, some level of corruption was standard practice. He reflected his times.

An enigma, Kiger loved his family, his community, and could be as tough a politician as he needed to be. He had many accomplishments. Carl Kiger was much more than just a murder victim.

---

[119] KY Post December 20, 1943

[120] KY Post August 20, 1943

[121] Cincinnati Times-Star August 19, 1943

[122] Interview with Gridley October 17, 2011

[123] KY Post August 9, 1922

www.ingramcontent.com/pod-product-compliance
Lightning Source LLC
Chambersburg PA
CBHW030024290326
41934CB00005B/474